AN OUTLINE OF
MODERN EUROPEAN HISTORY

An Outline of Modern European History

By

Halford L. Hoskins, Ph.D.

Professor of History, Tufts College

Garden City   New York
Doubleday, Page & Company
1925

COPYRIGHT, 1925, BY DOUBLEDAY, PAGE
& COMPANY. ALL RIGHTS RESERVED.
PRINTED IN THE UNITED STATES AT THE
COUNTRY LIFE PRESS, GARDEN CITY, N. Y.

FIRST EDITION

PREFACE

HISTORY should be more to the student than a mere succession of personages and events; it should have meaning, it should enlighten, as well. Although the whole truth of historical data can not often be arrived at, a course of historical study should afford as much interpretation of facts as modern historical criticism can offer. "The roots of the present lie deep in the past"; and unless history shows causation, unless it at least partially explains the significance of events, it has little practical value. Much of the meaning of history must be obtained from thoughtful reading, and it is the function of a study outline to guide such reading and to suggest its interpretation by means of both organization and terminology. The topics of the accompanying outline, therefore, have been arranged with a view to provoking thought and inquiry rather than to providing a complete synopsis of subject matter.

Furthermore, topics otherwise interesting but which would seem to bear no direct relation to the main theme of the present outline have been omitted. This has made possible the construction of a logical and consistent outline, which begins with a brief review of ancient times, introduces more detail as the subject progresses, and continues with constant *crescendo* to the present day. Very recent events, while often of great importance, are still so difficult of evaluation, that a more extended examination of them than that indicated in the outline would scarcely be profitable.

The topical material included in this study outline has therefore been selected with the object of showing origins, transitions, and movements—in a word, the lines of development of human institutions. To this end, it has not been practicable to adhere strictly to chronological treatment of the subject matter, but instead a topical method has been largely used, care being taken to preserve a feeling of historical continuity to the greatest possible degree. Thus, the main topics are arranged to show a general time sequence, while within these the unit topics are arranged in logical rather than in chronological fashion.

The author is fully sensible of the limitations of this or any other

Preface

study outline, but he believes that the present organization of the wide field is a practicable way of approaching the subject matter of European history. The outline is a by-product of the author's own teaching, and he ventures to believe that it may be found useful in courses where the emphasis is to be placed on the modern era.

Thanks are due to Mr. Josiah C. Russell, Instructor in History in Harvard University, for aid in verifying the references in the syllabus.

HALFORD L. HOSKINS.

MEDFORD HILLSIDE, MASS.
OCTOBER, 1925.

CONTENTS

	PAGE
PREFACE	v
SUGGESTIONS FOR HISTORY WORK IN COURSE	1
I. NOTEBOOK PREPARATION	1
II. HISTORY PAPERS OR THESES	3
III. TOPICS FOR PAPERS OR SPECIAL REPORTS	6
IV. BOOK REVIEWS	14
V. SUGGESTIONS FOR THE USE OF OUTLINE MAPS	15
BIBLIOGRAPHY	18
I. WORKS OF GENERAL CHARACTER	18
II. NATIONAL AND SECTIONAL HISTORIES	24
III. WORKS ON SPECIAL PHASES OF EUROPEAN HISTORY	29
OUTLINE OF MODERN EUROPEAN HISTORY	37

I. ELEMENTS IN WESTERN EUROPEAN HISTORY.
  A. THE COURSE OF HISTORY.
    1. Historical Attitude and Historical Perspective . . 37
    2. Contributions of the Ancients 38
  B. DECLINE OF CLASSICAL CIVILIZATION.
    3. The Barbarian Migrations: Social Fluidity . . . 39
    4. Guiding Influences of the Christian Church . . . 40
    5. The Challenge of Islam to the Western World . . 41
    6. The Carolingian Empire: Crystallizing Processes . . 42

II. MEDIEVAL DEVELOPMENT.
  A. THE REMOLDING OF EUROPE.
    7. The Evolution of the Feudal Order 44
    8. Creation of the French Monarchy 45
    9. Rise of the English Kingdom 46
    10. The Holy Roman Empire: the Universal State . . 47
  B. THE CLIMAX OF MEDIEVAL LIFE AND CULTURE.
    11. Organization and Functions of the Universal Church . 48
    12. The Crusades: Composite Enterprises 50
    13. Prevailing Economic and Social Conditions . . . 51
    14. Medieval Learning and Philosophy 52

Contents

PAGE

III. THE ERA OF THE RENAISSANCE.
A. THE EXPANDING OF HUMAN INTERESTS.
15. The Italian Background of the Renaissance . . . 53
16. Culture of the Renaissance Era 55
17. The Widening of European Horizons 56
B. MONARCHISTIC TENDENCIES IN EUROPEAN POLITICS.
18. The Evolution of Spain and Portugal 57
19. Asiatic Influences on Eastern Europe 58
20. Issues of the Hundred Years' War 59
21. Central Europe on the Eve of the Reformation . . 60

IV. THE REFORMATION AND POLITICAL READJUSTMENT.
A. BEGINNINGS OF THE PROTESTANT UPHEAVAL.
22. Religious Antecedents of the Reformation 61
23. The Lutheran Revolt 62
B. PROGRESS OF THE REFORMATION MOVEMENT.
24. The Epidemic Spread of Protestantism 63
25. The English Reformation 65
26. The Maintenance of English Independence . . . 66
C. RELIGIOUS AND POLITICAL READJUSTMENT.
27. Philip II and the Revolt of the Netherlands . . . 67
28. Dynastic and Religious Wars in France 68
29. The Thirty Years' War in Germany 69

V. EVOLUTION OF A EUROPEAN STATES SYSTEM.
A. ENGLISH EXPERIMENTS IN PERSONAL GOVERNMENT.
30. The Stuarts as "Divine Right" Rulers 70
31. Modified Republicanism: Commonwealth and Protectorate 71
32. The Restoration and the "Glorious Revolution" . . 72
B. THE ACCOMPANIMENTS OF DESPOTISM IN FRANCE.
33. Recovery of the French Monarchy 73
34. The Age of Louis XIV 74
C. CHANGES IN THE EUROPEAN POLITICAL FAMILY.
35. The Emergence of Russia 75
36. Origin and Rise of the Prussian Kingdom 76
37. Austria and the Extinction of Poland 77

VI. COMMERCIALISM AND THE NEW PHILOSOPHY.
A. STRUGGLES FOR COLONIAL SUPREMACY.
38. The Commercial Revolution 79
39. Beginnings of Colonial Expansion 80
40. The Colonial Duel of England and France 81
41. Revolution within the British Empire 82
B. THE PATH OF MODERN PROGRESS.
42. English Constitutional Development 83

Contents

	PAGE
43. Opening of the Age of Reason	84
44. The Eighteenth Century Scientific Movement	85
45. The *Ancien Régime*	86

VII. THE FRENCH REVOLUTIONARY CYCLE.
A. THE PERIOD OF THE REVOLUTION.
46. Beginnings of the French Revolution	88
47. The Trial of Limited Monarchy	89
48. Experiments with Democracy: the Convention	90

B. THE NAPOLEONIC PERIOD.
49. Formation of the Empire	91
50. Attempted Mastery of Europe	92
51. Decline and Fall of the Napoleonic Structure	93

VIII. ALTERNATING REACTION AND REVOLUTION.
A. THE PERIOD OF RETRENCHMENT.
52. The Revamping of Europe at Vienna	94
53. The "Concert" of Europe	96
54. The July Revolution in France	97
55. Revolutions beyond France in 1830	98

B. THE INDUSTRIAL REVOLUTION.
56. Modern Industrial Beginnings	99
57. Features of the Factory System	100

C. THE MID-CENTURY REVOLUTIONARY PERIOD.
58. The February Revolution of 1848	101
59. Revolutionary Movements in Central Europe	102
60. The Partial Triumph of Reaction	103

IX. THE CENTRIPETAL INFLUENCES OF NATIONALISM.
A. EMERGENCE OF THE ITALIAN NATION.
61. Accretional Origin of the Italian Kingdom	105
62. Consolidation of the Italian Nation	106
63. Recent National Issues in Italy	107

B. REALIGNMENT OF THE GERMAN STATES.
64. Prussian Assumption of German Leadership	108
65. Establishment of the German Empire	109

C. RECENT COURSE OF THE CENTRAL POWERS.
66. Early Progress of the German State	110
67. The Course of Pan-Germanism	111
68. Nationalism in the Hapsburg Monarchy	112

X. WAVES OF LIBERALISM AND DEMOCRACY.
A. THE RISE OF A DEMOCRATIC FRANCE.
69. The Second Napoleonic Empire	113
70. Early Vicissitudes of the Third Republic	114
71. French Problems in Democratic Government	116

Contents

                                                                                  PAGE

B. A CENTURY OF REFORM IN ENGLAND.
    72. Abolition of the Old Régime 117
    73. Extension of the Reform Movement. 118
    74. The Close of the Victorian Era 119
    75. Perfecting of Cabinet Government 120
C. DECLINE OF MEDIEVALISM IN RUSSIA.
    76. Autocratic Policies: Reform and Reaction 121
    77. Growth of Social and Political Unrest 122

XI. WORLD PROBLEMS AND ATTEMPTED SOLUTIONS.
  A. RECENT HISTORY OF THE NEAR EAST.
    78. Interests of the Powers in Balkan Liberation . . . 124
    79. The Turkish Revolution and the Balkan Wars. . . 125
  B. IMPERIALISM AND INTERNATIONAL DIPLOMACY.
    80. Scope of the British Empire 126
    81. Recent Phases of European Expansion 127
    82. The Balance of Power and the Alliances 129
    83. The Prelude to War: Diplomatic Clashes 130

XII. GROPING FOR A FINAL SOLUTION.
  A. THE WORLD WAR.
    84. Opening and Spread of the War 131
    85. Conduct of the War: Peace Efforts 132
    86. War-Time Revolutions 133
  B. PEACE AND PARTIAL RECONSTRUCTION.
    87. The Documentary Bases of Peace 134
    88. The Threatened Collapse of Europe 135
    89. The New World Map 136
    90. Symptoms of World Unrest 137

OUTLINE MAPS

                                                FOLLOWING PAGE

1. Human Inundations of Western Europe 10
2. Embryonic Beginnings of European States. 18
3. Rise of Christian Nation-States 26
4. Formation of European Languages 34
5. Economic Development of Europe 42
6. Era of Political Readjustment 50
7. World-Wide Expansion of Western Europe 58
8. Pre-Revolutionary Europe 66
9. French Revolutionary and Napoleonic Europe . . . 74
10. Europe after the Congress of Vienna 82
11. Industrial Europe 90
12. National Liberation and Unification 98
13. Colonialism and Imperialism 106
14. The World War 114
15. Europe since 1918 122
16. The New World 130

AN OUTLINE OF
MODERN EUROPEAN HISTORY

SUGGESTIONS FOR HISTORY WORK IN COURSE[1]

I. NOTEBOOK PREPARATION

It is very generally maintained that, for best results, the use of notebooks is essential in history work. It is, in any case, well established that poor notebooks and note-taking methods are often worse than none. The following proved methods will be found useful in obtaining good results.

1. **Size and Variety of Notebooks.** The notebook for history use should always be of the loose-leaf, side-opening variety, accommodating paper 5 by 8 inches, 6 by 9 inches, or $8\frac{1}{2}$ by 11 inches in size—these being standard filing sizes. The 5 by 8 inches size is recommended to students whose writing is of average size.

2. **Arrangement of Notes.** Only one side of the page should be used for note taking.

Notes may be written along the longer dimension of the sheet to good advantage. This contributes to the leaving of a substantial margin on the left-hand side of every sheet. This margin may be used for the noting of sources and pages of reading on which notes are based, and the main headings of topics on which notes are taken. The margin thus forms an index to the entire body of notes, and it should be used as such.

Notes should always be written in ink. Notes taken with pencil almost invariably blur, and frequently become illegible.

Notes may be taken in summary (paragraph) form or in outline form. The former is much to be preferred. If the latter style is used, the outline should be made to give actual information which will be of material assistance in reviewing the work.

A standard filing box or cabinet is recommended as a depository for notes as they are removed from the notebook. These may be easily indexed and kept for ready and permanent reference.[2]

---

[1] The author is indebted to the McKinley Publishing Company for permission to include here the substance of his article entitled, "Self-Starting the College Freshman History Course," which appeared in the *Historical Outlook* for October, 1923, pp. 254–257.

[2] See the article entitled, "Notes on Professional Cold Storage," in the *Historical Outlook* for June, 1922, pp. 205–207.

Notebook Preparation

A wide margin on the right-hand side of the note sheet is particularly valuable when work is being done involving any degree of research. This margin should be used for the student's comments on and interpretation of the notes on the body of the page, which are usually quotations, excerpts, or digests of important data. This margin should occupy perhaps one-fourth or more of the entire page, and when employed as suggested, it greatly simplifies the writing of papers or articles based on the notes taken.

3. **Content and Organization of Notes.** Notes in course will usually include:

   a. The main points, at least, in every class lecture,
   b. The main substance of prescribed reading,
   c. Selections of important material from recommended reading,
   d. Materials gathered in the independent investigation of a particular subject.

There should ordinarily be no duplication of materials. Marginal jottings (cross references) in the notebook will indicate more than one place where the same data may be found. Notes should ordinarily not be taken on textbook material, inasmuch as it is assumed that the text is always at hand for reference.

Notes should preferably be organized under the topic assigned for study, and should always indicate whether they are based on *lectures* or *collateral reading*.

The margins of note pages should, as a rule, show a complete record of the reading done outside of the textbook in connection with the subject.

4. **Value of the Notebook.** A number of purposes are served by the history notebook:

   a. It assists the memory process in concentrating attention on the materials written down.
   b. It functions as a synopsis of the subject and as a source of pertinent information in a rapid review of the ground covered.
   c. It preserves the "cream" of the work done in the subject for reference in subsequent years.
   d. It gives valuable practice in the organization, condensation, and composition of materials.

It is hardly necessary to point out to the conscientious student that a notebook reflects the character and habits of its owner, and is one of the most infallible indications of the student's attitude toward learning.

II. HISTORY PAPERS OR THESES

As a rule, broad courses in history do not admit of much special study or detailed investigation of the very many personalities, factors of environment, and events which history comprises. For that reason, it is a customary practice to give opportunity during a course for a careful and intensive investigation of one or more of the great variety of important points included in the field of study.

1. **The Undertaking: Choice of Subject.** The accompanying list of topics (see p. 6) is given to suggest the variety of subjects which can be profitably treated in this fashion. Those suggested are, for the most part, general in character. They will usually need to be further limited or defined for actual use, to conform to:

   a. The interests or purposes of the student,
   b. Books and materials available on the subject, and
   c. Space limits prescribed for the paper.

This defining of the subject is an important matter, and should not be undertaken without having given considerable thought to the nature, scope, and *historical significance* of the subject as listed.

It may be pointed out that the proper treatment of a biographical subject is not altogether a simple matter. In selecting a topic of this kind, one should not attempt to write a *biography* or a *life*, but to discuss the personage chosen from some particular historical point of view; that is, his relation to the important developments of his own or subsequent times.

2. **The Tools: Bibliography.** The next step in the preparation of the paper is the location and evaluation of all sources of information bearing on the subject. These should be classified thus:

   a. Primary (original) sources—official documents (laws, constitutions, decrees, etc.), contemporary papers, memoirs, accounts by eye-witnesses, etc.
   b. Secondary (derived) sources—books, papers, articles, etc., by more recent writers, based directly or indirectly on the above.

Materials in each list should be arranged *alphabetically* (by name of author), and the bibliography should show, for each work listed,

   a. Author's full name, reversed,
   b. Full title of the work,
   c. Place of publication (city and publishing house), and
   d. Date of publication, together with—
   e. A brief critical analysis or review of each title, showing its general nature and its fitness for use in connection with the particular subject.

History Papers or Theses

Magazine articles should be listed by author, whenever possible; otherwise by title of article. In either case, the name of the journal, volume number, and pages incorporating the article should be given.

3. **The Raw Material: Basic Information.** As reading on the subject progresses, careful notes should be taken on all materials which pertain particularly to the subject in hand. These notes may consist of excerpts or digests, or both. It is very important, however, that these notes, on which the paper itself is to be based, show definitely whence they were obtained, so that it will not be necessary to waste time and pains at the last in searching through materials once used in order to cite the source of authority in the final paper.

4. **Shaping of the Work: Outline.** When all sources of information are in hand and their content known, a preliminary or trial outline should be constructed, showing the form and proportions of the paper *as projected*. No hard and fast rules for the construction of outlines can be given. The following suggestions, however, should remove some of the difficulties.

   a. Determine the general parts into which the subject naturally or logically falls (usually somewhere between 3 and 8 in number for papers of this kind). Set these down, topically, as main headings.
   b. Determine the main considerations in each of these main divisions, and set them down, topically, as sub-topics—and so on, to perhaps the third stage of sub-division.
   c. Keep in mind, also, that when a topic is divided, it will be into at least two parts.
   d. The outline should be logical (*i.e.*, reasonable), and should reflect the proportions it is intended that the finished paper should have.

It may be well to confer with the Instructor regarding Bibliography and Outline before actually writing the paper.

5. **The Finished Product: Completed Manuscript.** History does not consist merely of facts; it involves an explanation or interpretation of these facts, as well. Hence, history has to be re-written for each generation. Each history paper or "thesis" should represent an attempt to contribute to the knowledge and understanding of the subject dealt with. It should be *original*—in method of approach, in analysis, in evaluation of sources, in historical interpretation. It should *not* copy or mimic.

The paper should, nevertheless, show the sources of the basic information drawn upon for *each important statement or allusion* in its text. These citations of authority should be inserted, along with

History Papers or Theses

any other parenthetical, critical, or explanatory notes desired, in footnotes, and should include:

a. Author,
b. Title,
c. Volume, and page or pages relating to the matter in hand.

The paper should be prepared in accordance with the rules and usages which obtain in ordinary English composition. Due care should be exercised with regard to unity and coherence (so that the theme or *thesis* may be always in evidence), and to the more mechanical matters of spelling, punctuation, paragraphing, margins, spacing, etc.

The following requisites, particularly, should be noted and followed in the manuscript to be submitted:

a. A title page, containing title of paper, name of author, number of course, and date submitted,
b. A *revised*, classified Bibliography,
c. A *revised* Outline, showing how the paper *has been* organized and written.

And the paper should be—

d. Typewritten, on one side of typewriter paper (approximately $8\frac{1}{2}$ by 11 inches in size),
e. In length, as specified by the Instructor,
f. Prepared in duplicate, so that one copy may be retained by the student.

6. **Abbreviations.** A number of abbreviations and formal, standard expressions are commonly used in writing and in printing for convenience and economy in valuable time and space. Some of those most frequently employed, with their English equivalents, which may be used to advantage in the preparation of history papers, follow. They are given here without capital letters: in actual use, capitals will naturally be employed in the usual manner.

art.—article
cf. (cp.)—compare
circa (ca.)—about
cit.—citation
ed. (s)—editor (s)
e.g.—for example
et seq. (sq., sqq.)—and the following
f. (ff.)— [page (s)] following
ibid. (ib., id.)—the same: in the same place

i.e.—that is
infra (in., infr.)—below
in loc.—in its (the same) place
i.q.—the same as
loc. cit.—in the place before cited
ms. (mss.)—manuscript (s)
n.—note
non seq.—it does not follow
op. cit.—previous citation
p. (pp.)—page (s)

Topics for Papers or Special Reports

passim—here and there
sc.—namely
seq. (sq., sqq.)—the following; next
u.s. (ut supra)—as above
viz.—namely; to wit
vol. (s)—volume (s)
supra (s., sup.)s—above
vide (v., vid.)—ee

III. TOPICS FOR PAPERS OR SPECIAL REPORTS

THE PERIOD OF RACIAL AND INSTITUTIONAL ORIGINS.

Phases of Religious Life.
1. Spread of Christianity in the Roman Empire.
2. The Council of Nicæa.
3. The Iconoclastic Controversy.
4. Religion of the Teutonic Barbarians.
5. Introduction of Christianity into Germany.
6. Organization of the Early Church in Britain.
7. Rise of the Temporal Power of the Papacy.
8. Character and Spread of Mohammedanism.

Political and Social Conditions.
9. Domestic Life of the German Barbarians.
10. Political Organization of the Early Germans.
11. Rise of the Frankish Kingdom.
12. Character of the Visigothic Kingdom.
13. Exploits of the Vandals.
14. Conquests of the Northmen.
15. The Code of Justinian.

CHARACTERISTICS OF THE MIDDLE AGES.

Church History.
16. The Dominican and Franciscan Orders.
17. The Cluniac Revival.
18. The Benedictine Order.
19. Causes of the Crusades.
20. The Latin Empire of Jerusalem.
21. The Order of Teutonic Knights.
22. Knights Templars and Knights Hospitallers.
23. The Children's Crusade.
24. The Albigensian Heresy.
25. Founding of the Society of Jesuits.
26. The Inquisition in Spain.
27. The Great Schism.
28. The Babylonian Captivity of the Papacy.

Medieval Trade and Commerce.
29. Medieval Trade Routes.
30. The Medieval Fair.
31. The Hanseatic League.
32. Nature of Medieval Commerce.

Topics for Papers or Special Reports

33. Causes of the Rise of Towns.
34. Craft and Merchant Gilds.

Political and Military History.
35. Struggles of Popes and Emperors.
36. The Lombard League.
37. *Magna Charta.*
38. Methods of Feudal Warfare.
39. Administration of Feudal Law and Justice.
40. Trial by Ordeal.
41. Mongol Conquests in Europe.
42. Beginnings of the English Parliament.
43. Organization and Equipment of Medieval Armies.
44. Medieval Town Government.
45. Evolution of the Feudal Castle.
46. Fall of the Eastern Roman Empire.

Medieval Life and Culture.
47. Origin of the Medieval Serf.
48. Moorish Life and Culture.
49. Medieval Farming Methods.
50. Life of the Feudal Nobility.
51. Rise of Chivalry.
52. Structure of Typical Monasteries.
53. Medieval Town Life.
54. Study of Medieval Science.
55. Effects of the Black Death.
56. Scholasticism.

Beginnings of Vernacular Literature in:
57. France.
58. Germany.
59. England.

EARLY MODERN TIMES.

The Renaissance Era.
60. Origin and Growth of Universities.
61. Causes of the Italian Intellectual Awakening.
62. Renaissance Art and Architecture.
63. Early History of the Printing Press.
64. Contributions of the Humanists.
65. Structure of Later Medieval Cathedrals.
66. Early Portuguese Explorations.

Era of the Reformation.
67. Church Councils Prior to the Reformation.
68. The Religious Situation in 16th-century Germany.
69. Religious Abuses of Luther's Time.
70. The Work of John Hus.
71. Teachings of John Calvin.
72. Property and Wealth of the Church.

Topics for Papers or Special Reports

SEVENTEENTH CENTURY EUROPE.

Reflections from the Religious Wars.
73. Effects of Race and Geography in the Netherlands.
74. The Union of Utrecht.
75. The Revocation of the Edict of Nantes.
76. Background of the Bohemian Revolt.
77. Military Campaigns of the Thirty Years' War.
78. Germany in 1648.
79. The Court of Louis XIV.

Political and Religious Struggles in England.
80. The Gunpowder Plot.
81. The Ulster Plantations.
82. Origin of the Petition of Right.
83. Trial and Execution of Charles I.
84. Political Structure of the Commonwealth.
85. The Religious Situation, 1640–1660.
86. *Annus Mirabilis.*
87. The "Glorious Revolution" of 1688.
88. Constitutional Importance of the Bill of Rights.

FEATURES OF EIGHTEENTH CENTURY EUROPE.

Central and Eastern Europe.
89. The Russian Church.
90. The Building of St. Petersburg (Leningrad).
91. Travels of Peter I.
92. Political and Social Reforms of Peter I.
93. Feudal Government of Poland.
94. The Diplomatic Revolution, 1748–1756.
95. Attempted Reforms of Joseph II (Austria).
96. The Partitions of Poland.
97. Growth of Brandenburg-Prussia.
98. Beginnings of the Decline of Turkey.

Developments in Western Europe.
99. The French Third Estate in the 18th Century.
100. Teachings of Rousseau.
101. The Domestic System in Industry.
102. Attempted Financial Reforms of Louis XVI.
103. Doctrines of Turgot and Adam Smith.
104. Results of the Seven Years' War.

Eighteenth Century England.
105. English Attitude toward the American Revolution.
106. Beginnings of Party Government in England.
107. Representation in Parliament before 1832.
108. Agriculture and Industry in England.
109. Characteristics of 18th Century English Literature.
110. Life and Manners in England.

Topics for Papers or Special Reports

111. Decline of Gilds in England.
112. Inventions Bringing in the Industrial Revolution.
113. Features of the New Factory System.

Commercialism and Colonialism.
114. Portuguese and Dutch Trading Monopolies in the East.
115. Organization and Government of the English East India Company.
116. The Character of Spanish Colonial Government.
117. Factors in the Growth in 18th Century Trade.
118. Effect of French Revolutionary and Napoleonic Wars on Hispanic America.
119. The Struggle for Mastery in India.

Biographical: The Personal Element in European History.
120. Alfred.
121. Charlemagne.
122. Hildebrand.
123. Mohammed.
124. Urban II.
125. Frederick Barbarossa.
126. Abelard.
127. The Medici.
128. Innocent III.
129. William the Conqueror.
130. Ridhard I.
131. Philip Augustus.
132. Henry Tudor (Henry VII).
133. Henry the Navigator.
134. Savonarola.
135. Martin Luther.
136. Ulrich Zwingli.
137. John Knox.
138. Wyclif and the Lollards.
139. Dante and His Work.
140. Michael Angelo.
141. Roger Bacon.
142. "Good Queen Bess."
143. Francis Drake.
144. Mary Stuart.
145. Charles V.
146. Philip II (Spain).
147. William the Silent.
148. Henry IV (Navarre).
149. Richelieu.
150. Mazarin.
151. Louis XIV.
152. Gustavus Adolphus.
153. Charles I (England).
154. Oliver Cromwell.
155. Frederick II (Prussia).

Topics for Papers or Special Reports

156. Peter I.
157. Maria Theresa.
158. Voltaire.
159. Francis Bacon.
160. William Pitt, The Younger.

THE FRENCH REVOLUTION AND NAPOLEON.

Period of the French Revolution.
161. Leaders of the National Assembly.
162. The Constitution of 1791.
163. Influence of Paris Mob on the Revolution.
164. The Estates General, 1302–1789.
165. Early Days of the French Revolution.
166. Origin of the Declaration of the Rights of Man.
167. The National Assembly and the Church.
168. The Failure of the Constitution of 1791.
169. Revolutionary Political Clubs in France.
170. The Reign of Terror.
171. Problems and Accomplishments of the Directory.

The Napoleonic Régime.
172. Napoleon's Egyptian Campaign.
173. The Constructive Works of Napoleon in France.
174. Napoleon's Military Policy.
175. The Reorganization of Germany.
176. The Continental System.
177. The Treaties of Tilsit.
178. The Russian Campaign.
179. The Peninsular Campaign.
180. The Imperial Court of Napoleon.
181. Abolition of Feudalism by Napoleon.
182. The Hundred Days.
183. Personnel of the Congress of Vienna.
184. The European Treaties of 1814.

THE RISE OF THE POPULAR VOICE.

The Era of Metternich.
185. Accomplishments of the Vienna Congress.
186. The German Confederation.
187. The Holy Alliance.
188. Revolutionary Movements of 1820.
189. Suppression of Ideas in Germany.

Nineteenth Century Revolution.
190. The July Revolution in France.
191. The War of Greek Independence.
192. The Belgian Revolution.
193. The Great Reform Bill in England.
194. The February Revolution in France.

Topics for Papers or Special Reports

195. Revolution and Reaction in Austria.
196. Revolution and Repression in Hungary.
197. The Frankfort Convention.
198. Cross Currents in Italy, 1848–1849.
199. Polish Revolutions in the 19th Century.

NATIONAL UNIFICATION AND NATIONAL DEVELOPMENT.

The Rise of New Nation-States.
200. The Italian *Resorgimento*.
201. Foreign Policy of Cavour.
202. The *Carbonari*.
203. Italian Unification, 1859–1861.
204. *Italia Irredenta*.
205. The *Zollverein* as a Basis for German Unification.
206. Bismarck as a "Parliament Tamer."
207. Causes and Effects of the Seven Weeks' War.
208. Responsibility for the Franco-German War.
209. Origin and Nature of the German Imperial Government.

National Problems of Great Britain.
210. Repeal of the Corn Laws.
211. Rise of Trades Unions.
212. Home Rule for Ireland.
213. English Constitutional Changes, 1866–1885.
214. Development of Public Education.

Political Evolution of France and Italy.
215. Liberalism under Napoleon III.
216. The "Commune" of 1870.
217. Genesis of the Third French Republic.
218. Constitution of the Third Republic.
219. The Dreyfus Case.
220. The Meaning of *Fascismo* in Italy.
221. Relation of Church and State in Italy.

The Germanic States.
222. Growth of Militarism in the German Empire.
223. Alsace-Lorraine Under German Rule.
224. Socialism and Social Legislation in Germany.
225. The Schleswig-Holstein Problem.
226. The *Kulturkampf*.
227. Austro-Hungarian Relations after 1848.
228. The Nationalities of Austria-Hungary before 1914.

Russia.
229. Functions of the Russian *Mir*.
230. Nihilism and Terrorism.
231. Effects of the Abolition of Serfdom.
232. The Industrial Revolution in Russia.
233. The Coöperative Movement in Russia.
234. The Russian Revolution.

Topics for Papers or Special Reports

EUROPEAN COLONIAL EXPANSION AND IMPERIALISM.

The British Empire.
235. Projects for British Imperial Federation.
236. British Penetration into Mesopotamia.
237. The Suez Canal as a Factor in British Expansion.
238. The Opening up of Africa.
239. British Mandates since 1918.
240. The Anglo-Indian Trade.
241. Factors in the Sepoy Mutiny.
242. Causes of the Present Indian Unrest.

Phases of Continental European Expansion.
243. Italian Emigration to the New World.
244. German Colonization in Brazil.
245. The *Bagdadbahn.*
246. Belgian Maladministration in the Congo.
247. Russian Expansion into Siberia.
248. European Spheres of Influence in China.
249. French Indo-China.
250. The Relation of Trade to Colonial Expansion.
251. Colonial Interests as War Incentives in 1914.
252. Awards of the Mandates Commission.

The Highway to the Far East.
253. Building and Control of the Suez Canal.
254. Anglo-Russian Interests in Persia.
255. British Political Control in Egypt.
256. Cyprus, 1876–1925.
257. British Penetration into Mesopotamia.
258. The Lausanne Conference.

The Decline of Turkey.
259. Factors in the Crimean War.
260. The Turkish Constitution of 1876.
261. The Young Turk Movement.
262. The Congress of Berlin, 1878.
263. Diplomacy of the Balkan Wars of 1912 and 1913.
264. Establishment of the Angora Government.
265. The Greek Disaster in Asia Minor.
266. Constantinople as the Focus of European Diplomacy.

Late Diplomatic History.
267. Formation of the Triple Alliance.
268. Evolution of the Triple Entente.
269. Accomplishments of the Hague Peace Conferences.
270. The Austro-Serbian Controversy.
271. The European Expedition to China, 1900.
272. The Fashoda Incident.
273. Franco-German Clashes over Morocco.
274. Meaning of the Anglo-Japanese Alliance.

Topics for Papers or Special Reports

THE WORLD WAR AND POST-WAR PROBLEMS.

War-Time Developments.
275. "The Freedom of the Seas."
276. The Treaty of Brest-Litovsk.
277. Influence of the "Fourteen Points."
278. The German Revolution.
279. War-Time Government in Britain.
280. Effects of the War on the Mohammedan World.

Recent Movements.
281. Accomplishments of the League of Nations.
282. Consequences of the Versailles Treaty.
283. Occupation of the Ruhr.
284. Settlement of the Silesian Question.
285. The Meaning of Bolshevism.
286. Work of the Washington Conference on Armaments.
287. Indications of a Trend toward Normalcy.
288. Persian Oil as a Disturbing Influence.
289. The "Dawes Plan" of German Reparation.
290. Causes of Unrest in European Colonial Possessions.

Biographical: The Personal Element.
291. Louis XVI.
292. Lafayette.
293. Marat.
294. Danton.
295. Robespierre.
296. Napoleon Bonaparte.
297. Josephine Beauharnais (Bonaparte).
298. The Duke of Wellington.
299. Talleyrand.
300. Prince Metternich.
301. Alexander I (Russia).
302. Cavour.
303. Garibaldi.
304. Mazzini.
305. Louis Blanc.
306. Karl Marx.
307. Palmerston.
308. Sir Robert Peel.
309. Napoleon III.
310. Bismarck.
311. Kossuth.
312. Victoria.
313. Disraeli.
314. Gladstone.
315. Livingstone.
316. Abdul Hamid II.

Book Reviews

317. Wilhelm II.
318. Clemenceau.
319. Lloyd George.
320. General Smuts.

IV. BOOK REVIEWS

Nowhere more than in the study of history does the student need a "critical, questioning spirit." A useful exercise which cannot fail in giving better appreciation of the element of bias, that is, the personal element, in the writing of history, and which may be considered a mild form of historical criticism, is that of the reviewing of books containing historical subject matter.

Book reviewing has been made something of a fine art by those who write reviews for the general public. Gems of the reviewer's art may be found in almost any literary journal; but excellent examples of critical reviews of historical works are contained in the *American Historical Review, Historical Outlook, History, English Historical Review, Political Science Quarterly*, and other publications of the same variety. For such reviews as these, no set rules can be given. However, the essentials of a critical review may be gathered from reference to the following outline.

1. THE BOOK: ADVERTISEMENT.
    a. The author: experience and training qualifying him for his task.
    b. The title in full, with subtitles.
    c. Place and date of publication or latest revision; the publisher; size of book.

2. HISTORICAL AND LITERARY CONTENT.
    a. General organization of the whole and of particular phases of the field or subject.
    b. Proportions devoted to industry, social conditions, war, law, government and diplomacy, with reference to the stated object of the book.
    c. Accuracy and adequacy of the subject matter, with regard to the character and number of sources bearing on the subject.
    d. Style of literary treatment and sentence structure: note for what group of readers the book is intended.

3. AMPLIFICATIVE AND SUPPLEMENTARY FEATURES.
    a. Notes, comments, and citations of authority: location and value.
    b. Character, number, location and classification of reference books.
    c. Character and number of maps, charts and plans: consider as aids to visualization.
    d. Illustrations: criticize as to their historical accuracy and their supplementing of the text material.
    e. Character and utility of summaries, appendices, and index.

Suggestions for the Use of Outline Maps

4. SUMMARY OF FAVORABLE AND UNFAVORABLE CRITICISMS.
   a. Practicability of the book with reference to its intended purpose.
   b. Its value relative to other works in the same field or subject.
   c. Its specific contributions.

V. SUGGESTIONS FOR THE USE OF OUTLINE MAPS

The difficulty of teaching the great truths of history is the principal reason for the widespread belief that history is "hard" or "dry," for the subject matter itself is essentially interesting. Anything, then, which contributes to the visualization of historical facts and factors performs a definite service in the learning process.

One of the methods commonly employed as an aid to visualization is the use of outline maps. A map is a conventionalized diagram, representing the whole, or a part, of the earth's surface. Maps may be used to indicate almost innumerable conditions: location, direction, distance, area, control, natural resources, manufacturing output, trade conditions, lands and distribution of populations, social statistics, etc., etc.

Maps are therefore specialized for historical purposes, map outlines being prepared to show area, or proportion, or direction, as the case may be, and the diagram or projection prepared accordingly. The outline map should, therefore, be selected according to the purpose to be served.

The advantages in the use of outline maps are several:

   a. They insure accuracy in outlines and proportions of land and water areas,
   b. They reduce the time required in the teaching of essential locations and relationships, and
   c. They furnish bases for tests of historical knowledge.

A technique in the preparation of outline maps should be determined upon at the outset and maintained throughout the course. The materials generally used in preparing maps are colored pencils or crayons, water colors, and colored inks. The inks are probably to be preferred.

It is usually not necessary to have the entire map colored: the results are likely to be inartistic, and too much time is required if more than the salient points are delineated.

The suggestions in the following list are given to indicate a few of the several ways in which the outline maps interspersed throughout this book may be employed.[1] These maps may be prepared to show

---

[1] In preparing these map studies, data will need to be drawn in many instances from text accounts. Maps in Turner and in other text and reference books may also be referred to, and for many details the student should consult one or more of the atlases mentioned in the Bibliography, page 35.

Suggestions for the Use of Outline Maps

any one of the features here proposed, or several of them, or other phases of European development not mentioned.

1. HUMAN INUNDATIONS OF WESTERN EUROPE (*Following page* 10). Boundaries and provinces of the old Roman Empire; routes of barbarian migrations; Mohammedan conquests; physical features of Europe; the spread of Christianity; etc.

2. EMBRYONIC BEGINNINGS OF EUROPEAN STATES (*Following page* 18). The founding of Germanic kingdoms: Franks, Normans, Lombards, Saxons, etc.; the Empire of Charlemagne; the Spanish marches; the Partition of Verdun; etc.

3. RISE OF CHRISTIAN NATION-STATES (*Following page* 26). Development of France and England; routes of the Crusades; location of important churches and monasteries; the Holy Roman Empire; Papal dominion; etc.

4. FORMATION OF EUROPEAN LANGUAGES (*Following page* 34). Rise of French, Spanish, Portuguese, Italian, German tongues and their dialects; lines of demarcation between Germanic and Romance languages with reference to political boundaries; language boundaries between German and Slavs; etc.

5. ECONOMIC DEVELOPMENT OF EUROPE (*Following page* 42). Medieval trade routes and fairs; spheres of commercial organizations; centers and kinds of manufacturing; relation between roads and towns; population distribution and density; etc.

6. ERA OF POLITICAL READJUSTMENT (*Following page* 50). The evolution of German states; Europe after the Peace of Westphalia; changes in the Netherlands and in Italy; rise of the Hapsburg domain; contested boundaries; non-Christian Europe; etc.

7. WORLD-WIDE EXPANSION OF WESTERN EUROPE (*Following page* 58). Fifteenth and Sixteenth Century explorations; way stations and slaving grounds; areas of settlement; development of colonies; results of colonial wars; etc.

8. PRE-REVOLUTIONARY EUROPE (*Following page* 66). Rise of Prussia; partitions of Poland; political results of Eighteenth Century wars; routes of campaign and sites of important battles; etc.

9. FRENCH REVOLUTIONARY AND NAPOLEONIC EUROPE (*Following page* 74). Europe in 1789, 1802, 1810; the re-making of Italy and Germany; alliances against Napoleon; the continental blockade; principal campaigns; states controlled by and allied with France; etc.

10. EUROPE AFTER THE CONGRESS OF VIENNA (*Following page* 82). The map of 1815—buffer states, territorial compensations to the Allies, French boundaries; the contrast of political and language frontiers; the Quadruple and Quintuple Alliances; etc.

11. INDUSTRIAL EUROPE (*Following page* 90). Deposits of coal, iron, and other minerals; forest areas; railway and canal systems; agricultural production; manufacturing areas; growth of populations; etc.

12. NATIONAL LIBERATION AND UNIFICATION (*Following page* 98). The unification of Italy; *Italia Irredenta;* the *Zollverein;* integration of the German states; Alsace-Lorraine; rise of independent Balkan states; etc.

Suggestions for the Use of Outline Maps

13. COLONIALISM AND IMPERIALISM (*Following page* 106). Colonial empires of European states; protectorates and spheres of influence; strategic posts and naval bases; main routes of trade; disputed territories; oil fields; etc.

14. THE WORLD WAR (*Following page* 114). The Triple Entente and Triple Alliance; the "danger spots" of Europe; strategic railways; mobilization centers; fleet and submarine operations; battle zones and critical campaigns; areas of munitions production; battle lines on November 11, 1918; etc.

15. EUROPE SINCE 1918 (*Following page* 122). New boundaries of the Central Powers; the break-up of Austria-Hungary and Russia; rise of new states; compensations of territory to Entente Powers; the Ruhr situation; contested areas and plebiscites; rise of dictatorships; members of the League of Nations; etc.

16. THE NEW WORLD (*Following page* 130). Mandated areas; internationalized zones; new colonial areas and new states; naval and aërial bases; post-war hostilities; non-European members of the League of Nations; etc.

BIBLIOGRAPHY

The brief list of books given below is intended to be suggestive and stimulating, but it is not to be considered in any sense complete. Confined as it is almost entirely to well-known standard works in English, it has been selected to include a considerable variety of works on the many different phases of the history of Europe. It may therefore serve as an indication of the kinds and the nature of materials to which the student should have constant access during the study of the subject. Extensive acquaintance with the literature of the subject is one of the great *desiderata* of a course in history; and the study of the development of European peoples should lead to the investigation of many other materials which cannot profitably be incorporated in a general reading list of this kind. This Bibliography, therefore, bears much the same relationship to the literature on European history that the accompanying Outline does to the subject matter itself.

In preparing this list, preference has been given to publications of recent date as against older works, since the more recent publications usually have a better point of view and have the advantage of recent historical investigation. Some of the older historical works, however, possess so much of local color or excellence that they cannot be overlooked in the formation of any bibliography covering this field. The dates given are those of latest revision or copyright, as far as they can be ascertained. The original dates of publication of some of the older books are shown in parentheses.

I. WORKS OF GENERAL CHARACTER

A. ADVANCED TEXTS AND GENERAL ACCOUNTS.

1. The Early or Medieval Era.
  Adams, G. B.—*Civilization during the Middle Ages.* New York, (1894), 1914.
  Bémont, Ch. and Monod, A.—*Medieval Europe.* New York, 1902.
  Bryce, Jas.—*The Holy Roman Empire.* New York & London, 1923.
  Davis, H. W. C.—*Mediæval Europe.* New York, 1911.
  Emerton, E.—*Mediæval Europe.* Boston, 1903.
  Emerton, E.—*The Beginnings of Modern Europe, (1250–1450).* Boston, &c., 1917.
  Funck-Brentano, F.—*The Middle Ages.* (Trans.) New York, 1923.
  Munro, D. C. and Sellery, G. C.—*Medieval Civilization: Selected Studies from European Authors.* . . . New York, (1907), 1920.

Bibliography

MUNRO, D. C.—*The Middle Ages, 395-1272.* New York, 1921.
SEIGNOBOS, CH.—*A History of Mediæval and Modern Civilization.* New York, 1907.
STILLÉ, C. J.—*Studies in Mediæval Europe.* (Phila., 1882), New York, 1907.
SWINTON, Wm.—*Outlines of the World's History.* New York, (1874), 1902.
THATCHER, O. J. AND MCNEAL, E. H.—*Europe in the Middle Age.* New York, (1896), 1920.
THORNDIKE, L.—*History of Medieval Europe.* Boston, &c., 1920.

2. *The Modern Era.*
ANDREWS, C. M.—*The Historical Development of Modern Europe.* 2 vols. London, 1899.
DYER, T. H.—*A History of Modern Europe.* London, 1901.
FYFFE, C. A.—*A History of Modern Europe, 1792-1878.* Pop. ed., New York, 1896.
HAYES, C. J. H.—*A Political and Social History of Modern Europe.* 2 vols. New York, 1918, 1924.
HAZEN, C. D.—*Modern Europe.* New York, 1920.
LODGE, R.—*A History of Modern Europe.* . . . New York, 1886.
ROBINSON, J. H.—*An Introduction to the History of Western Europe.* (Brief ed.) Boston, 1925.
ROBINSON, J. H.—*An Introduction to the History of Western Europe.* 2 vols. Boston, 1924–
ROBINSON, J. H. AND BEARD, C. H.—*The Development of Modern Europe.* 2 vols. Boston, 1907, 1908.
SEIGNOBOS, CH.—*History of Contemporary Civilization.* New York, 1909.
TURNER, E. R.—*Europe, 1450-1789.* Garden City, 1923.
TURNER, E. R.—*Europe Since 1789.* Garden City, 1924.
WAKEMAN, H. O.—*Europe, 1598-1715.* New York, (1894), 1922.

3. *Comprehensive Works and Historical Series.*
Cambridge Mediæval History. 4 vols. London & New York, 1911-23. (In progress).
Cambridge Modern History. 14 vols. Cambridge (Eng.), 1902–1912.
GIBBON, E.—*Decline and Fall of the Roman Empire.* 7 vols. (J. B. Bury, Ed.) London, 1914.
HELMOLT, H. F.—*History of the World.* 9 vols. New York, 1904.
History of All Nations. 24 vols. Philadelphia. 1905.
HODGKIN, T.—*Italy and Her Invaders.* 8 vols. Oxford, 1892-1899.
LAVISSE, E. ET RAMBAUD, A.—*Histoire Générale*, 12 vols. Paris, 1893–1901.
SYMONDS J. A.—*The Renaissance in Italy.* 5 parts in 7 vols. New York, 1887-8.

B. WORKS ON SHORTER PERIODS.

1. *The Medieval Era.*
   a. The Period of Transition.
   BURY, J. B.—*History of the Later Roman Empire.* 2 vols. London, (1889), 1923.

Bibliography

EMERTON, E.—*Introduction to the Study of the Middle Ages.* Boston, 1903.
FERRERO, G.—*The Ruin of the Ancient Civilization and the Triumph of Christianity.* (Trans.) New York & London, 1921.
FREEMAN, E. A.—*Western Europe in the Fifth Century.* London, 1904.
HASKINS, C. H.—*The Normans in European History.* Boston & New York, 1915.
MAWER, A.—*The Vikings.* Cambridge (Eng.) & New York, 1913.
OMAN, C. W. C.—*The Dark Ages, 476-918.* New York & London, 1919.
SERGEANT, L.—*The Franks.* New York & London, 1898.
TAYLOR, H. O.—*The Classical Heritage of the Middle Ages.* New York, 1911.
VILLARI, P.—*The Barbarian Invasion of Italy.* 2 vols. London, 1902.

b. The Feudal Period.

ARCHER, T. A. AND KINGSFORD, C. L.—*The Crusades.* . . . New York. 1906.
BALZANI, U.—*The Popes and the Hohenstaufen.* London &c., 1901.
BARKER, E.—*The Crusades.* London, 1923.
BURY, J. B.—*A History of the Eastern Roman Empire.* New York, 1912.
COX, G. W.—*The Crusades.* New York, (1874), 1895.
CUTTS, E. L.—*Scenes and Characters of the Middle Ages.* London & New York (1872), 1925.
FISHER, H. A. L.—*The Mediæval Empire.* 2 vols. London, 1898.
FREEMAN, E. A.—*Western Europe in the Fifth Century.* . . . London, 1904.
HASKINS, C. H.—*Studies in the History of Mediæval Science.* Cambridge (Mass.), 1924.
HEARNSHAW, F. J. C.—*Mediæval Contributions to Modern Civilization.* London, 1921.
HENDERSON, E. F.—*A History of Germany in the Middle Ages.* London, 1894.
LEA, H. C.—*A History of the Inquisition of the Middle Ages.* 3 vols. New York, 1887.
LODGE, R.—*The Close of the Middle Ages, 1272-1494.* London & New York, 1922.
MAITLAND, F. W.—*Political Theories in the Middle Ages.* London, 1900.
OMAN, C. W. C.—*The Story of the Byzantine Empire.* New York & London, 1892.
SEIGNOBOS, CH.—*The Feudal Régime.* New York, 1908.
SEIGNOBOS, CH.—*The Mediæval Régime.* New York, 1902.
TAYLOR, H. O.—*The Mediæval Mind.* 2 vols. New York, 1914.
TOUT, T. F.—*The Empire and the Papacy, 918-1273.* London & New York, 1921.
ZIMMERN, HELEN—*The Hansa Towns.* New York, 1895.

Bibliography

2. The Early Modern Era.
   a. Renaissance and Reformation.
      BURCKHARDT, J.—*The Civilization of the Renaissance in Italy.* London, (1878), 1921.
      FISHER, G. P.—*The Reformation.* New York, (1873), 1905.
      HULME, E. M.—*The Renaissance, The Protestant Revolution and the Catholic Reformation.* . . . New York, 1923.
      JOHNSON, A. H.—*Europe in the Sixteenth Century, 1494–1598.* London, 1922.
      LINDSAY, T. M.—*A History of the Reformation.* 2 vols. New York, 1922.
      RANKE, L. VON—*History of the Reformation in Germany.* New York & London, (1844), 1905.
      SEEBOHM, F.—*The Era of the Protestant Revolution.* New York, (1874), 1920.
      SMITH, PRESERVED—*The Age of the Reformation.* New York, 1920.
      TANNER, E. M.—*The Renaissance and Reformation.* . . . Oxford, 1908.
      VEDDER, H. C.—*The Reformation in Germany.* New York, 1914.
      WALKER, W.—*The Protestant Reformation.* New York, 1902.
   b. The Seventeenth and Eighteenth Centuries.
      BOURGEOIS, E.—*The Century of Louis XIV.* London, 1896.
      GARDINER, *The Thirty Years' War, 1618–1648.* New York & London, 1891.
      HASSAL, A.—*The Balance of Power, 1715–1789.* London, 1914.
      JOHNSON, A. H.—*The Age of the Enlightened Despot, 1660–1789.* London, 1910.
      LOWELL, E. J.—*The Eve of the French Revolution.* Boston, 1899.
      PERKINS, J. B.—*France under the Regency.* Boston, 1920.
      TAINE, H. A.—*The Ancient Régime.* New York, (1876), 1896.
      WAKEMAN, H. O.—*Europe, 1598–1715.* New York, 1922.
   c. The French Revolution and Napoleon.
      BOURNE, H. E.—*The Revolutionary Period in Europe.* New York, 1914.
      CARLYLE, T.—*The French Revolution,* 3 vols. New York. (1838), 1909.
      HAZEN, C. D.—*The French Revolution and Napoleon.* New York, 1917.
      HAZEN, C. D. AND OTHERS.—*Three Peace Congresses of the Nineteenth Century.* Cambridge (Mass.), 1919.
      MADELIN, L.—*The French Revolution.* New York, 1923.
      MALLET, C. E.—*The French Revolution.* New York, 1913.
      MATHEWS, S.—*The French Revolution.* New York, 1923.
      ROSE, J. H.—*The Revolutionary and Napoleonic Era, 1789–1815.* Cambridge (Eng.), 1907.
      SEELEY, J. R.—*A Short History of Napoleon I.* Boston, 1901.
      STEPHENS, H. M.—*Revolutionary Europe, 1789–1815.* London & New York, 1907.
      WEBSTER, C. K.—*The Congress of Vienna, 1814–1815.* London, 1920.

Bibliography

3. **The Nineteenth and Twentieth Centuries.**
  a. Textbooks of General Scope.
  BOWMAN, I.—*The New World.* Yonkers-on-Hudson, 1922.
  FUETER, E.—*World History, 1815–1920.* (Trans.) New York, 1922.
  HAYES, C. J. H.—*A Political and Social History of Modern Europe.* Vol. II. New York, 1924.
  HAZEN, C. D.—*Europe Since 1815.* New York, 1923. (Also in a 2-vol. edition.)
  JUDSON, H. P.—*Europe in the Nineteenth Century.* New York, 1908.
  KIRKPATRICK, R. A.—*Lectures on the History of the Nineteenth Century.* Cambridge (Eng.), 1902.
  LIPSON, E.—*Europe in the Nineteenth Century: an Outline History.* London, 1916.
  PHILLIPS, W. A.—*Modern Europe, 1815–1899.* New York & London, 1903.
  ROBINSON, J. H.—*An Introduction to the History of Western Europe.* Vol II. Boston, 1925.
  ROBINSON, J. H. AND BEARD, C. H.—*The Development of Modern Europe.* Vol. II. Boston, 1908.
  SCHAPIRO, J. S.—*Modern and Contemporary European History.* Boston, 1922.
  SCHEVILL, F.—*A Political History of Modern Europe.* New York, 1921.
  SEIGNOBOS, CH.—*A Political History of Europe Since 1814.* New York, 1900.
  TURNER, E. R.—*Europe Since 1789.* Garden City, 1924.
  b. The Early Nineteenth Century.
  BLANC, L.—*History of Ten Years, 1830–1840.* 2 vols. London, 1844–1845.
  CRESSON, W. P.—*The Holy Alliance.* . . . New York, 1922.
  DICKINSON, G. L.—*Revolution and Reaction in Modern France.* London, 1892.
  EGERTON, H. E.—*British Foreign Policy in Europe.* . . . London, 1918.
  HALL, SIR J. R.—*England and the Orleans Monarchy.* London, 1912.
  HART, A. B.—*The Monroe Doctrine: An Interpretation.* Boston, 1917.
  MARRIOTT, J. A. R.—*The French Revolution of 1848 in Its Economic Aspect.* . . . 2 vols. Oxford, 1913.
  MARRIOTT, J. A. R.—*Remaking of Modern Europe, 1789–1878.* London, 1910.
  PAXSON, F. L.—*The Independence of the South American Republics.* Philadelphia, 1916.
  PHILLIPS, W. A.—*The Confederation of Europe.* . . . London & New York, 1920.
  ROSE, J. H.—*The Rise and Growth of Democracy in Great Britain.* Chicago, 1898.
  WALPOLE, S.—*Foreign Relations.* London, 1882.

Bibliography

C. RECENT TIMES IN EUROPE.

1. *Origins of the World War.*
    ANDERSON, F. M. AND HERSHEY, A. S.—*Handbook for the Diplomatic History of Europe, Asia, and Africa, 1870–1914.* Washington, 1918.
    BECK, J. M.—*The Evidence in the Case.* New York, 1915.
    CHITWOOD, O. P.—*The Immediate Causes of the Great War.* New York, 1918.
    CHOATE, J. H.—*The Two Hague Conferences.* Princeton, 1913.
    COOLIDGE, A.C.—*Origins of the Triple Alliance.* New York, 1917.
    DAVIS, W. S.—*The Roots of the War.* New York, 1918.
    HAZEN, C. D.—*Fifty Years of Europe.* New York, 1919.
    HOLT, L. H. AND CHILTON, A. W.—*The History of Europe from 1862 to 1914.* New York, 1918.
    GIBBONS, H. A.—*The New Map of Europe, 1911–1914.* New York, 1918.
    GOOCH, G. P.—*History of Modern Europe, 1878–1919.* New York, 1923.
    MARRIOTT, J. A. R.—*Europe and Beyond: A Preliminary Survey of World Politics in the Last Half Century.* New York, 1921.
    POWERS, H. H.—*The Things Men Fight For.* New York, 1916.
    ROSE, J. H.—*The Development of the European Nations, 1870–1921.* New York & London, 1922.
    ROSE, J. H.—*The Origins of the War, 1871–1914.* New York, 1922.
    SCHMITT, B. E.—*England and Germany, 1740–1924.* Princeton, 1916.
    SEYMOUR, CH.—*The Diplomatic Background of the War, 1870–1914.* New Haven, 1916.
    TARDIEU, A.—*France and the Alliances.* New York, 1908.
    TOYNBEE, A. J.—*Nationality and the War.* London & New York, 1915.
    WILLOUGHBY, W. W.—*Prussian Political Philosophy.* New York, 1918.

2. *The War and Its Conduct.*
    BASSETT, J. S.—*Our War with Germany.* New York, 1919.
    BRANDES, G.—*The World at War.* New York, 1917.
    BULLARD, A.—*The Diplomacy of the Great War.* New York, 1916.
    GIBBS, SIR P.—*Now It Can Be Told.* New York, 1920.
    HAYES, C. J. H.—*A Brief History of the Great War.* New York, 1922.
    HEADLAM, S. W.—*The History of Twelve Days—July 24 to August 4, 1914.* New York, 1915.
    JASTROW, M.—*The War and the Bagdad Railway.* Philadelphia, 1918.
    MCMASTER, J. B.—*The United States and the World War.* New York, 1920.
    MCPHERSON, W. L.—*A Short History of the Great War.* New York, 1920.
    OGG, F. A. AND BEARD, C. A.—*National Governments and the World War.* New York, 1919.
    POLLARD, A. F.—*A Short History of the Great War.* London, 1920.
    SIMONDS, F. H.—*History of the Great War.* 5 vols. Garden City, 1919–1920.

Bibliography

3. Europe Since the Treaty of Versailles.
BEARD C. A.—*Cross Currents in Europe To-day.* Boston, 1922.
BRANFORD, V. AND GEDDES, P.—*The Making of the Future.* London, 1917.
BRYCE, JAS.—*International Relations.* New York, 1922.
CHAPMAN, S. J.—*Labour and Capital after the War.* London, 1918.
GIBBS, SIR P.—*More That Must Be Told.* New York, 1921.
GIBBONS, H. A.—*The New Map of Asia.* New York, 1919.
HASKINS, C. H. AND LORD, R. H.—*Some Problems of the Peace Conference.* Cambridge (Mass.), 1922.
IRWIN, W.—*The Next War.* New York, 1921.
KEYNES, J. M.—*Economic Consequences of the Peace.* New York, 1920.
KEYNES, J. M.—*A Revision of the Treaty.* New York, 1922.
LANSING, R.—*The Peace Negotiations: a Personal Narrative.* Boston, 1921.
MOULTON, H. G. AND BASS, J. F.—*America and the Balance Sheet of Europe.* New York, 1922.
POWERS, H. H.—*The Great Peace.* New York, 1918.
SCOTT, W. R.—*Economic Problems of Peace After War.* Cambridge (Eng.), 1918.
TARDIEU, A.—*The Truth about the Treaty.* Indianapolis, 1922.
TOYNBEE, A. J.—*The New Europe.* . . . London & New York, 1916.
VANDERLIP, F. A.—*What Next in Europe?* New York, 1922.
ZIMMERN, A. E.—*Europe in Convalescence.* New York, 1922.

II. NATIONAL AND SECTIONAL HISTORIES

A. WORKS ON WESTERN EUROPEAN NATIONS.

1. Britain and the British Commonwealth.
a. Histories of Great Britain.
CHEYNEY, E. P.—*A Short History of England.* Boston, 1919.
CROSS, A. L.—*A History of England and Greater Britain.* New York, 1914.
GREEN, J. R.—*A Short History of the English People.* New York, &c., 1904.
HULME, E. M.—*History of the British People.* New York, 1924.
LARSON, L. M.—*History of England and the British Commonwealth.* New York, 1924.
LOW, S.—*The Governance of England.* New York, 1920.
LOWELL, A. L.—*The Government of England.* New York, 1917.
MARRIOTT, J. A. R.—*England Since Waterloo.* New York, 1922.
SLATER, G.—*The Making of Modern England.* Boston, &c., 1920.
STUBBS, W.—*The Constitutional History of England.* 3 vols. Oxford, (1878), 1903–1906.
TOUT, T. F.—*A History of Great Britain.* London & New York, 1920.
TREVELYAN, G. M.—*British History in the Nineteenth Century (1782–1901).* New York, 1922.

Bibliography

b. Histories of Ireland.
BARKER, E.—*Ireland in the Last Fifty Years.* New York, 1919.
PLUNKETT, SIR H.—*Ireland in the New Century.* London, 1904.
SMITH, G.—*Irish History and the Irish Question.* New York, 1905.

c. The British Empire.
BARNARD, H. CLIVE (ED.)—*The Expansion of the Anglo-Saxon Nations.* London, 1920.
BEER, G. L.—*The English Speaking Peoples.* . . . New York, 1918.
MUIR, R.—*A Short History of the British Commonwealth.* 2 vols. Yonkers-on-Hudson, 1922.
ROBINSON, H.—*The Development of the British Empire.* Boston, 1922.
SEELEY, SIR J. R.—*The Expansion of England.* Boston, (1891), 1921.
WILLIAMSON, J. A.—*A Short History of British Expansion.* London, 1923.
WOODWARD, W. H.—*A Short History of the Expansion of the British Empire.* Cambridge (Eng.), (1899), 1921.

2. France.
ADAMS, G. B.—*Growth of the French Nation.* London & New York, (1896), 1922.
BOURGEOIS, E.—*History of Modern France, 1815-1913.* Cambridge (Eng.), 1919.
BRACQ, J. C.—*France under the Third Republic.* New York, 1910.
BUELL, R. L.—*Contemporary French Civilization in the Nineteenth Century.* New York, 1920.
COUBERTIN, BARON PIERRE DE—*France Since 1814.* London, 1900.
DIMNET, E.—*France Herself Again.* London, 1914.
EVANS, DR. T. W.—*The Second French Empire.* (Ed. by Dr. E. A. Crane.) New York, 1905.
GUERARD, A. L.—*French Civilization in the Nineteenth Century.* New York, 1914.
HASSAL, A.—*France, Mediæval and Modern.* Oxford, 1918.
HAZEN, C. D.—*Alsace-Lorraine under German Rule.* New York, 1917.
MACDONALD, J. R. M.—*A History of France.* 3 vols. New York, 1915.
MASSON, G.—*Story of Mediæval France.* New York, 1893.
POINCARÉ, R.—*How France Is Governed.* London, 1914.
VIZETELLY, E. A.—*The True Story of Alsace-Lorraine.* London, 1918.

3. Germany.
a. The Rise of Prussia.
Dow, E. F.—*Outline of Prussian History to 1871.* Oxford, 1915.
MARRIOTT, J. A. R. AND ROBERTSON, C. G.—*The Evolution of Prussia.* . . . Oxford, 1917.
REDDAWAY, W. F.—*Frederick the Great and the Rise of Prussia.* New York, 1911.

b. The German States and the Empire.
BARKER, J. E.—*The Foundations of Germany.* New York, 1916.
BARKER, J. E.—*Modern Germany: Her Political and Economic Problems.* New York, 1912.

Bibliography

BÜLOW, B. H. M. K. VON—*Imperial Germany.* New York, 1917.
DAWSON, W. H.—*The Evolution of Modern Germany.* New York, 1914.
DAWSON, W. H.—*The German Empire, 1867-1914.* 2 vols. New York, 1919.
HENDERSON, E. F.—*A Short History of Germany.* 2 vols. New York, 1920.
HOWARD, B. E.—*The German Empire.* New York, 1906.
KRUGER, F. K.—*The Government and Politics of the German Empire.* Yonkers-on-Hudson, 1915.
MALLESON, G. B.—The Refounding of the German Empire. London, 1904.
SCHEVILL, F.—*The Making of Modern Germany.* Chicago, 1916.
SYBEL, H. von—*The Founding of the German Empire.* 7 vols. New York, 1890-1898.
YOUNG, G.—*The New Germany.* New York, 1920.

4. *Italy.*
DILLON, E. J.—*From the Triple to the Quadruple Alliance.* . . . New York, 1915.
JAMISON, E. M. AND OTHERS.—*Italy, Medieval and Modern.* Oxford, 1919.
KING, B.—*A History of Italian Unity, 1814-1871.* 2 vols. London, 1899.
KING, B. AND OAKLEY, T.—*Italy To-day.* London, 1901.
LATIMER, E. W.—*Italy in the Nineteenth Century.* Chicago, 1898.
LOW, S. J. M.—*Italy in the War.* New York, 1917.
THAYER, W. R.—*The Dawn of Italian Independence.* 2 vols. Boston, 1899.
TITTONI, T.—*Modern Italy: Its Intellectual, Cultural and Financial Aspects.* New York, 1922.
UNDERWOOD, F. M.—*United Italy.* London, 1912.
WALLACE, W. K.—*Greater Italy, 1858-1918.* New York, 1918.

5. *The Hispanic States.*
   a. Spain.
   CHAPMAN, C. E.—*History of Spain.* New York, 1918.
   HUME, M. A. S.—*Modern Spain, 1788-1898.* New York, 1909.
   HUME, M. A. S.—*Spain: Its Greatness and Decay (1479-1788).* Cambridge (Eng.), 1905.
   LANE-POOLE, S.—*The Moors in Spain.* New York, 1911.
   RICHMAN, I. B.—*The Spanish Conquerors.* New Haven, 1920.
   WATTS, H. E.—*The Christian Recovery of Spain.* New York, 1901.
   b. Portugal.
   CRAWFORD, O.—*Portugal, Old and New.* New York, 1882.
   KOEBEL, W. H.—*Portugal, Its Land and People.* London, 1909.
   OLIVEIRA MARTINS, J. P.—*The Golden Age of Prince Henry the Navigator.* London, 1914.
   STEPHENS, H. M.—*The Story of Portugal.* New York, 1903.
   YOUNG, G.—*Portugal, Old and Young.* Oxford, 1917.

Bibliography

6. *The Smaller Nations of Western Europe.*
BAIN, R. N.—*Scandinavia: The Political History of Denmark, Norway, and Sweden, from 1513 to 1900.* Cambridge (Eng.), 1905.
BLOK, P. J.—*History of the People of the Netherlands.* 5 vols. New York, 1898–1912.
BOULGER, D. C.—*A History of Belgium.* London, 1925.
BROOKS, R. C.—*The Government and Politics of Switzerland.* Yonkers-on-Hudson, 1921.
ENSOR, R. C. K.—*Belgium.* London, 1915.
HARVEY, W. J. AND REPPIEN, C.—*Denmark and the Danes.* London, 1915.
MACDONELL, J. C.—*Belgium, Her Kings, Kingdom and People.* Boston, 1914.
MCCRAKAN, W. D.—*The Rise of the Swiss Republic.* New York, 1901.
MOTLEY, J. L.—*History of the United Netherlands.* 4 vols. New York, (1856), 1909.
MOTLEY, J. L.—*Rise of the Dutch Republic.* 3 vols. New York, 1883.
NILSSON, V.—*Sweden.* New York & London, 1901.

B. HISTORIES OF CENTRAL AND EASTERN EUROPE.

1. *Russia.*
ALEXINSKY, G.—*Modern Russia.* New York, 1914.
BAIN, R. N.—*Slavonic Europe.* . . . Cambridge (Eng.), 1908.
BEAZLEY, R., FORBES, N. AND BIRKETT, G. A.—*Russia from the Varangians to the Bolsheviks.* Oxford, 1918.
CURTIN, J.—*The Mongols in Russia.* Boston, 1908.
DILLON, E. J.—*The Eclipse of Russia.* London, 1918.
HINDUS, M.—*The Russian Peasant and the Revolution.* New York, 1920.
KORFF, BARON S. A.—*Russia's Foreign Relations During the Last Half Century.* New York, 1922.
KORNILOV, A.—*Modern Russian History.* . . . 2 vols. New York, 1924.
LEVINE, I. D.—*The Russian Revolution.* New York, 1917.
MAVOR, J.—*An Economic History of Russia.* New York, 1914.
MORFILL, W. R.—*History of Russia.* New York, 1902.
ROSS, E. A.—*Russia in Upheaval.* New York, 1918.
SKRINE, F. H.—*The Expansion of Russia, 1815–1900.* New York, 1915.
WALLACE, W. R.—*History of Russia.* New York, 1902.

2. *Austria-Hungary.*
DRAGE, G.—*Austria-Hungary.* London, 1909.
GAYDA, V.—*Modern Austria: Racial and Social Problems.* New York, 1915.
SETON-WATSON, R. W.—*Racial Problems in Hungary.* London, 1908.
STEED, H. W.—*The Hapsburg Monarchy.* New York, 1914.
WHITMAN, S.—*Austria.* New York, 1899.
WHITMAN, S.—*The Realm of the Hapsburgs.* New York, 1905.

Bibliography

3. The Balkans.
  a. General Treatises.
  DAVIS, W. S.—*A Short History of the Near East.* . . . New York, 1923.
  FORBES, N., AND OTHERS—*The Balkans: a History.* Oxford, 1915.
  MARRIOTT, J. A. R.—*The Eastern Question.* New York, 1918.
  MILLARD, T. F. F.—*Our Eastern Question.* New York, 1916.
  MILLER, W.—*The Balkans: Roumania, Bulgaria, Servia and Montenegro.* New York, 1911.
  MOWRER, P. S.—*Balkanized Europe.* New York, 1923.
  NEWBIGIN, M. I.—*Geographical Aspects of Balkan Problems.* . . . London, 1915.
  SCHEVILL, F.—*The History of the Balkan Peninsula.* New York, 1922.
  SCHURMAN, J. G.—*The Balkan Wars.* Princeton, 1916.
  SETON-WATSON, R. W.—*The Rise of Nationality in the Balkans.* London, 1916.
  VILLARI, L.—*The Balkan Question.* . . . London, 1905.
  b. The Rise of Balkan States.
  BRAILSFORD, H. N.—*Macedonia: Its Races and Their Future.* London, 1906.
  CLARK, C. U.—*Greater Roumania.* New York, 1922.
  DAKO, C. A.—*Albania, The Master Key to the Near East.* Boston, 1919.
  DEVINE, A.—*Montenegro in History, Politics and War.* London, 1918.
  MILLER, W.—*A History of the Greek People (1821–1921).* London, 1922.
  PEACOCK, W.—*Albania: the Foundling State of Europe.* New York, 1914.
  PHILLIPS, W. A.—*The War of Greek Independence, 1821–1833.* New York, 1897.
  PROTIĆ, S.(Balkanicus)—*The Aspirations of Bulgaria.* London, 1915.
  SERGEANT, L.—*Greece in the 19th Century.* London, 1897.
  SETON-WATSON, R. W.—*Roumania and the Great War.* London, 1915.
  TEMPERLEY, H. W. V.—*History of Serbia.* London, 1919.
  WACE, A. J. B. AND THOMPSON, M. S.—*The Nomads of the Balkans.* London, 1914.

4. Turkey and the Ottoman Empire.
  ABBOTT, G. F.—*Turkey in Transition.* London, 1909.
  CREASY, SIR E. S.—*Turkey.* (Ed. by A. C. Coolidge and W. H. Claflin.) New York, 1913.
  EVERSLEY, LORD AND CHIROL, SIR V.—*The Turkish Empire from 1288 to 1922.* New York, 1923.
  LANE-POOLE, S.—*The Story of Turkey.* New York, 1888.
  MARRIOTT, J. A. R.—*The Eastern Question: an Historical Study in European Diplomacy.* Oxford, 1918.
  MILLER, W.—*The Ottoman Empire and Its Successors.* Cambridge (Eng.), 1923.
  PEARS, SIR E.—*Turkey and Its People.* London, 1912.
  TOYNBEE, A. J.—*Turkey: A Past and a Future.* New York, 1917.

Bibliography

5. *Minor Eastern States.*
BENEŠ, E.—*Bohemia's Case for Independence.* London, 1917.
FISHER, J. R.—*Finland and the Tsars.* London, 1899.
GIBBONS, H. A.—*The Reconstruction of Poland and the Near East.* . . . New York, 1917.
GRUBER, DR. J.—*Czechoslovakia: A Survey of Economic and Social Conditions.* (Trans.) New York, 1924.
MORFILL, W. R.—*The Story of Poland.* New York, 1903.
ORVIS, J. S.—*A Brief History of Poland.* Boston, 1916.
READE, A.—*Finland and the Finns.* New York, 1917.
RUDNICKI, S.—*The Ukraine.* Jersey City, 1915.
RUDNITSKY, S.—*Ukraine: The Land and Its People.* New York, 1918.
RUHL, A. B.—*New Masters of the Baltic.* New York, 1921.

III. WORKS ON SPECIAL PHASES OF EUROPEAN HISTORY

A. HISTORICAL FACTORS, INSTITUTIONS, AND MOVEMENTS.

1. *Political, Economic and Social Conditions.*
CHEYNEY, E. P.—*Introduction to the Industrial and Social History of England.* New York, 1922.
CUNNINGHAM, W.—*The Growth of English Industry and Commerce.* 2 vols. Cambridge (Eng.), 1912.
CUNNINGHAM, W.—*The Industrial Revolution.* Cambridge (Eng.), 1908.
DAY, C.—*A History of Commerce.* New York, (1907), 1922.
DRAPER, J. W.—*History of the Intellectual Development of Europe.* 2 vols. New York & London, 1905.
FISHER, H. A. L.—*The Republican Tradition in Europe.* London, 1911.
GIBBINS, H. DE B.—*Industry in England.* New York, (1896), 1920.
GRAHAM, M. W.—*New Governments of Central Europe.* New York, 1924.
HOBSON, J. A.—*The Evolution of Modern Capitalism.* London & New York, 1902.
INNES, A. D.—*England's Industrial Development.* London, 1912.
LOWELL, A. L.—*Greater European Governments.* Cambridge (Mass.), 1925.
MACGREGOR, D. H.—*The Evolution of Industry.* New York, 1918.
MUNRO, W. B.—*The Governments of Europe.* New York, 1925.
OGG, F. A.—*Governments of Europe.* New York, (1896), 1920.
OGG, F. A.—*The Economic Development of Modern Europe.* New York, 1922.
ORTH, S. P.—*Socialism and Democracy in Europe.* New York, 1913.
PERRIS, G. H.—*The Industrial History of Modern England.* New York, 1914.
POLLARD, A. F.—*Factors in Modern History.* New York, 1907.
SPARGO, J.—*Socialism.* . . . New York & London, 1906.
TICKNER, F. W.—*Social and Industrial England.* New York, 1920.

Bibliography

TOYNBEE, A.—*Lectures on the Industrial Revolution 18th Century in England.* London, (1887), 1912.
WEBSTER, W. C.—*A General History of Commerce.* Boston, (1903), 1918.
WHELPLEY, J. D.—*The Trade of the World.* New York, 1915.
USHER, A. P.—*The Industrial History of England.* Boston, 1920.

2. *The European Expansion Process.*
ABBOTT, W. C.—*The Expansion of Europe.* 2 vols. New York, 1924.
BOLTON, H. E. AND MARSHALL, T. M.—*The Colonization of North America, 1492–1783.* New York, 1920.
BOURNE, E. G.—*Spain in America, 1450–1580.* New York & London, 1906.
CHEYNEY, E. P.—*The European Background of American History.* New York & London, 1904.
DOUGLAS, R. K.—*Europe and the Far East.* Cambridge (Eng.), 1924.
FISKE, J.—*The Discovery of America.* 2 vols. Boston & New York, 1892.
FULLERTON, W. M.—*Problems of Power,* New York, 1920.
GIBBONS, H. A.—*The New Map of Africa, 1900–1916.* . . . New York, 1916.
HARRIS, N. D.—*Intervention and Colonization in Africa.* Boston, 1914.
HOBSON, J. A.—*Imperialism, a Study.* New York, 1905.
IRELAND, A.—*Tropical Colonization.* New York, 1899.
JEBB, R.—*Studies in Colonial Nationalism.* London, 1905.
JOHNSTON, SIR H. H.—*History of the Colonization of Africa by Alien Races.* Cambridge (Eng.), 1913.
KELLER, A. G.—*Colonization.* Boston, 1908.
KELTIE, J. S.—*The Partition of Africa.* London, 1895.
MERRIMAN, R. B.—*Rise of the Spanish Empire.* . . . 2 vols. New York, 1918.
MORRIS, H. C.—*History of Colonization.* 2 vols. New York, 1904.
MUIR, R.—*The Expansion of Europe.* Boston, 1923.
ORTH, S. P.—*The Imperial Impulse.* . . . New York, 1916.
REINSCH, P. S.—*Colonial Government.* New York, 1916.

3. *The Factors of Geography, Race, and Language.*
BRUNHES, J.—*Human Geography.* Chicago, 1920.
CHAMBERLAIN, H. S.—*Foundations of the 19th Century.* New York, 1914.
DIXON, R. B.—*The Racial History of Man.* New York, 1923.
DOMINIAN, L.—*Frontiers of Language and Nationality in Europe.* New York, 1917.
DUCKWORTH, W. L. H.—*Prehistoric Man.* Cambridge (Eng.), 1912.
FAIRGREVE, J.—*Geography and World Power.* New York, 1921.
FEBVRE, LUCIEN—*A Geographical Introduction to History.* (Trans.) New York, 1925.
FLEURE, H. J.—*Human Geography in Western Europe.* London, 1918.
FREEMAN, E. A.—*The Historical Geography of Europe.* London & New York, 1903.
GOLDENWEISER, A. A.—*Early Civilization: An Introduction to Anthropology.* New York, 1922.

Bibliography

GRANT, M.—*The Passing of the Great Race.* New York, 1922.
HADDON, A. C.—*The Wanderings of Peoples.* Cambridge (Eng.), 1912.
HUNTINGTON, E—*The Character of Races, as Influenced by Physical Environment.* New York, 1924.
MCCABE, J.—*The Evolution of Civilization.* New York, 1922.
MILL, H. R.—*The International Geography.* New York, 1907.
RIPLEY, W. Z.—*The Races of Europe: a Sociological Study.* New York, 1915.
ROSE, J. H.—*Nationality in Modern History.* New York, 1916.
SEMPLE, E. C.—*Influences of Geographic Environment.* . . . New York & London, 1911.
TOYNBEE, A. J.—*Nationality and the War.* . . . London & Toronto, 1915.
WHITNALL, H. O.—*The Dawn of Mankind.* Boston, 1924.

B. GUIDES AND ILLUSTRATIVE MATERIALS.

1. Works on History and Historiography.
a. Guides to Historical Reading.
AMERICAN HISTORICAL ASSOCIATION—*A Guide to Historical Literature.* (Ed. by Dutcher and Others). *In preparation.*
ANDREWS, C. M., GAMBRILL, J. N. AND TALL, L.—*A Bibliography of History for Schools and Libraries.* New York, 1910.
CANNON, H. L.—*Reading References for English History.* Boston, 1910.
DAHLMANN-WAITZ, G.—*Quellenkunde der Deutschen Geschichte.* Leipzig, 1912.
GROSS, C.—*The Sources and Literature of English History.* New York & London, 1915.
KERNER R. J.—*Slavic Europe.* Cambridge (Mass.), 1918.
MOLINIER, A.—*Les Sources de l'histoire de France.* 6 vols. Paris, 1901-1906.
PAETOW, L. J.—*Guide to the Study of Medieval History.* Berkeley, 1917.
PIRENNE, H.—*Bibliographie de l'histoire de Belgique.* Bruxelles, 1902.
b. Historical Method and Criticism.
BARNES, H. E.—*The New History and the Social Studies.* New York, 1925.
BERNHEIM, E.—*Exposition of Historic Method.* (Trans.) Leipzig, 1894.
CROCE, B.—*History—Its Theory and Practice.* (Trans.) New York, 1923.
DROYSEN, J. G.—*Outline of the Principles of History.* (Trans.) Boston, 1893.
FLING, F. M.—*The Writing of History: An Introduction to Historical Method.* New Haven, 1920.
FREEMAN, E. A.—*The Methods of Historical Study.* London, 1886.
LAMPRECHT, K.—*What Is History?* (Trans.) New York, 1905.
LANGLOIS, C. V. AND SEIGNOBOS, CH.—*Introduction to the Study of History.* (Trans.) New York, (1898), 1925.

Bibliography

ROBINSON, J. H.—*The New History.* New York, 1912.
SHOTWELL, J. T.—*An Introduction to the History of History.* New York, 1922.
TEGGART, F. J.—*Prolegomena to History.* Berkeley, 1916.

2. *Source Materials.*
ANDERSON, F. M.—*The Constitutions and Other Select Documents Illustrative of French History.* Minneapolis, 1908.
BEER G. L.—*African Questions at the Paris Peace Conference.* . . . New York, 1923.
CHEYNEY, E. P.—*Readings in English History.* Boston, 1922.
COLBY, C. W.—*Selections from the Sources of English History.* London, New York, &c., 1899.
FRESKA, FREDERICK (Comp.)—*A Peace Congress of Intrigue (Vienna, 1815).* (Trans.) New York, 1919.
GREAT BRITAIN, FOREIGN OFFICE—*Collected Diplomatic Documents Relating to the Outbreak of the European War.* London, 1915.
HAYES, C. J. H.—*British Social Politics.* . . . Boston, New York, &c., 1913.
HENDERSON, E. F.—*Select Historical Documents of the Middle Ages.* London & New York, 1892.
HERTSLET, SIR E.—*Map of Europe by Treaty.* 4 vols. London, 1875–1891.
HOLLAND, T. E.—*The European Concert in the Eastern Question: a Collection of Treaties.* Oxford, 1885.
MCBAIN, H. L. AND ROGERS, L.—*The New Constitutions of Europe.* Garden City, 1923.
MCKINLEY, A. E.—*Collected Materials for the Study of the War.* Philadelphia, 1918.
OGG, F. A.—*A Source Book of Mediæval History.* . . . New York, &c., 1908.
ROBINSON, J. H.—*Readings in European History.* 2 vols. Boston, New York, &c., 1904–1906.
ROBINSON, J. H. AND BEARD, C. A.—*Readings in Modern European History.* 2 vols. Boston, 1908–1909.
SCOTT, J. B. (Ed.)—*Autonomy and Federation within Empire.* Washington, 1921.
SCOTT, J. B. (Ed.)—*Diplomatic Documents Relating to the Outbreak of the European War.* 2 vols. Oxford, 1916.
SPEARE, M. E. and Norris, W. B.—*World War Issues and Ideals.* Boston, 1918.
THATCHER, O. J. AND MCNEAL, E. H.—*Source Book for Mediæval History.* New York, 1905.
UNIVERSITY OF PENNSYLVANIA—*Translations and Reprints.* 6 vols. Philadelphia & New York, 1909.
YOUNG, ARTHUR—*Travels in France During the Years 1787, 1788, 1789.* (Ed. by M. Bentham–Edwards). London, 1889.

Bibliography

3. Biography.
  a. Medieval Times.
    DAVIS, H. W. C.—*Charlemagne.* New York, 1900.
    EINHARD—*The Life of Charlemagne.* New York, 1915.
    FREEMAN, E. A.—*William the Conqueror.* London & New York, 1888.
    HODGKIN, T.—*Charles the Great.* London, 1912.
    HODGKIN, T.—*Theodoric the Goth.* New York, 1894.
    HOWORTH, H. H.—*St. Gregory the Great.* London, 1912.
    LARSON, L. M.—*Canute the Great.* New York, 1912.
    PLUMMER, C.—*The Life and Times of Alfred the Great.* Oxford, 1902.
    PROTHERO, G. W.—*The Life of Simon de Montfort.* London, 1877.
  b. Early Modern Times.
    BEAZLEY, C. R.—*Prince Henry the Navigator.* New York, 1897.
    BEESLY, E. S.—*Queen Elizabeth.* New York, 1906.
    BELLOC, H.—*Robespierre.* New York, 1901.
    CARLYLE, T.—*Frederick the Great.* London, 1884.
    CESARESCO, COUNTESS E. M.—*Cavour.* New York, 1898.
    CREIGHTON, M.—*The Age of Elizabeth.* London, (1876), 1897.
    GARDINER, S. R.—*Oliver Cromwell.* London, 1901.
    HASSAL, A.—*Louis XIV and the Zenith of the French Monarchy.* New York & London, 1904.
    HUME, M. A. S.—*Philip II of Spain.* London, 1911.
    JACOBS, H. E.—*Martin Luther, The Hero of the Reformation.* New York & London, 1902.
    LODGE, R.—*Richelieu.* London & New York, 1908.
    MACAULAY, T. B.—*Essays* on Clive, Hastings, Frederick the Great, Madame d'Arblay.
    MALLESON, G. B.—*Robert Clive.* London, 1895.
    MORLEY, J.—*Rousseau.* New York & London, (1873), 1922.
    MORLEY, J.—*Voltaire.* New York, (1872), 1905.
    PERKINS, J. B.—*Richelieu.* New York, 1901.
    SMITH, P.—*The Life and Letters of Martin Luther.* Boston & New York, 1911.
    THACHER, J. B.—*Christopher Columbus.* 3 vols. New York, 1903-1904.
    YOUNG, N.—*The Life of Frederick the Great.* New York, 1919.
  c. Recent Times.
    FISHER, H. A. L.—*Napoleon.* London, 1921.
    FOURNIER, A.—*Napoleon the First.* New York, 1911.
    HEADLEM, J. W.—*Bismarck and the Founding of the German Empire.* New York, (1899), 1914.
    JOHNSTON, R. M.—*Napoleon, a Short Biography.* New York, 1904.
    KEBBEL, T. E.—*Life of Lord Beaconsfield.* London, 1888.
    KING, B.—*Mazzini.* London, 1902.
    MACAULAY, T. B.—*Essay on William Pitt,* in *Essays, Critical and Miscellaneous.* Philadelphia, 1854.
    MADELIN, L.—*Danton.* (Trans.) New York, 1921.
    MONYPENNY, W. F. AND BUCKLE, G. E.—*The Life of Benjamin Disraeli.* 6 vols. New York, 1910-1920.

Bibliography

MORLEY, J. M.—*The Life of William Ewart Gladstone.* 2 vols. New York, (1903), 1911.
ROBERTSON, C. G.—*Bismarck.* New York, 1919.
ROSE, J. H.—*The Life of Napoleon I.* 2 vols. New York, 1924.

4. Historical Fiction.

BLACKMORE, R. D.—*Lorna Doone.* (Seventeenth Century England).
BLASCO IBAÑEZ, V.—*The Four Horsemen of the Apocalypse.* (The Great War).
BUCHAN, J.—*Greenmantle.* (Period of the Great War).
BULWER-LYTTON, SIR E.—*The Last of the Barons.* (Rise of the English Commons).
COOPER, J. F.—*The Spy.* (Anglo-French Struggles in America).
DAVIS, W. S.—*God Wills It.* (The First Crusade).
DAVIS, W. S.—*The Friar of Wittenberg.* (The German Reformation).
DICKENS, CH.—*Tale of Two Cities.* (French Revolution).
DOYLE, A. C.—*The Refugees.* (France under Louis XIV).
DOYLE, A. C.—*The White Company.* (Medieval England).
DUMAS, A.—*The Three Musketeers.* (France under Richelieu).
ELIOT, G.—*Adam Bede.* (English Village Life).
ELIOT, G.—*Romola.* (Italy: time of Savonarola).
GOGOL, N. V.—*Dead Souls.* (Modern Russia).
HARDY, A. S.—*Passe Rose.* (Period of the Migrations).
HARRISON, F.—*Theophano.* (Spread of Mohammedanism).
HUGO, V.—*Les Misérables.* (The French Revolution).
HUGO, V.—*Notre Dame.* (The Rise of Medieval France).
KINGSLEY, CH.—*Hypatia.* (Later Roman Empire).
KINGSLEY, CH.—*Westward Ho!* (A Tale of Elizabethan Seamen).
MEREZHKOVSKII, D. S.—*Romance of Leonardo da Vinci.* (The Italian Renaissance).
READE, CH.—*The Cloister and the Hearth.* (Fifteenth Century England.)
SABATINI, R.—*Scaramouche.* (The French Revolution).
SCHEFFEL, J. V.—*Ekkehard.* (Exploits of the Normans).
SCOTT, SIR W.—*Ivanhoe.* (Thirteenth Century England).
SCOTT, SIR W.—*Quentin Durward.* (France in the Fifteenth Century).
SCOTT, SIR W.—*The Talisman.* (The Crusades).
SIENKIEWICZ, H.—*Quo Vadis?* (Early Christian Persecution).
THACKERAY, W. M.—*Henry Esmond.* (English Life in the Eighteenth Century).
TOLSTOY, A. K.—*The Terrible Czar.* (Rise of Russia).
WALLACE, L.—*Ben Hur.* (The Eastern Roman Empire).
WATERLOO, S.—*The Story of Ab.* (Prehistoric Times).
WELLS, C.—*In the Reign of Queen Dick.* (Cromwellian England).
WELLS, H. G.—*Mr. Britling Sees It Through.* (The Great War).
WHITE, E. L.—*Andivius Hedulio.* (The Later Roman Empire).
ZOLA, E.—*The Downfall.* (End of the Second French Empire).

Bibliography

5. *Atlases.*
   BATHOLOMEW, J. G.—*An Atlas of Economic Geography.* Oxford, 1914.
   BARTHOLOMEW, J. G.—*An Atlas of European History, 1789–1918.* Oxford, 1919.
   Dow, E. W.—*Atlas of European History.* New York, 1909.
   FINCH, V. C. AND BAKER, O. E.—*Geography of the World's Agriculture.* Washington, D. C., 1917.
   HEARNSHAW, F. J. C.—*Macmillan's Historical Atlas of Modern Europe.* London, 1920.
   MUIR, R.—*Hammond's New Historical Atlas.* New York, 1914.
   PUTZGER, F. W.—*Historischer Schul-Atlas.* . . . Leipzig & New York, 1923.
   SHEPHERD, W. R.—*An Historical Atlas.* New York, 1921.
   Universal Atlas of the World. Chicago (Rand, McNally), 1914.

AN OUTLINE OF MODERN EUROPEAN HISTORY

ALTHOUGH the accompanying syllabus has been arranged with particular reference to Professor E. R. Turner's *Europe, 1450–1789* and *Europe Since 1789*, it will be noted that it is designed to permit ready correlation with a number of the better texts.

The "Parallel References" given under each unit topic of the syllabus are as nearly as possible of equal length and scope, though there is necessarily considerable variation in the historical value of these accounts. In any case, there is an individual difference in point of view, which makes desirable the reading of more than one of the parallel references in connection with the text account before the readings in the more detailed works listed under "Supplementary References" are taken up. These supplementary readings, selected from a wide range of works on various subjects, frequently do not cover the whole of a lesson topic. They give detailed information on some of the major points in the lesson topic, however, and serve to indicate to some extent the vast field of historical literature from which one may draw. "Source Readings" are, naturally, selections from the primary or original sources of history, and are valuable for illustrative purposes.

Other titles than those listed in the Bibliography, bearing on one part or another of the course, may be readily found by referring to bibliographical guides, classified card catalogues, chapter bibliographies in text and reference books (such as the Cambridge histories), encyclopedias (*Encyclopædia Britannica*), book catalogues, publishers' lists, and the like. Articles in historical publications and current literature may be discovered by examining the indexes of the publications likely to contain pertinent materials, or, better, by referring to such guides to periodical literature as *Poole's Index* or the current *Reader's Guide*.

I. ELEMENTS IN WESTERN EUROPEAN HISTORY

A. THE COURSE OF HISTORY.

   1. **Historical Attitude and Historical Perspective.**
     a. Definition of History.
        i. The subject matter.
       ii. The relation of history to the sciences.
       iii. The approach to history: historical criticism.

2. Contributions of the Ancients

b. The Continuity of History.
  i. The relation of history to prehistory.
  ii. Cycles in human development: chronology.
c. The Practical Importance of History.
  i. The bases of history.
    (a) The factor of heredity.
    (b) Environment and its influences.
  ii. Sources of historical knowledge.
  iii. Methods of historical study.
  iv. The philosophy of history: present-day application.

Turner, *Europe, 1450-1789*, pp. 1-3.

Parallel References:
ADAMS, *Civilization During the Middle Ages*, ch. 1.
EMERTON, *Introduction to the Middle Ages*, pp. xi–xviii.
ROBINSON, *History of Western Europe*, I, pp. 1–16.
ROBINSON, *Introduction to the History of Western Europe*, (brief ed.), pp. 1–7.
SCHEVILL, *Political History of Modern Europe*, Introduction.
SWINTON, *Outlines of History*, Introduction, sec. I, ch. 1.
THATCHER AND MCNEAL, *Europe in the Middle Age*, Introduction.
THORNDIKE, *History of Medieval Europe*, ch 1.

Supplementary References:
CROCE, *History: Its Theory and Practice*, pt. I, chs. 1–4, 7, 9; DAVIS, *Medieval Europe*, Introduction; DROYSEN, *Outline of the Principles of History*; GRANT, *Passing of the Great Race*, pt. I, ch. 2; pt. II, chs. 4–6; LANGLOIS AND SEIGNOBOS, *Introduction to the Study of History*, bks. I–II; MILL, *The International Geography*, ch. 11; RIPLEY, *The Races of Europe*, chs. 1, 2, 6; ROBINSON, *The New History*, ch. 1; SEMPLE, *The Influence of Geographic Environment*; SHOTWELL, *Introduction to the History of History*, chs. 1–4, 27; TEGGART, *Prolegomena to History*, ch. 5, *passim*.

2. **Contributions of the Ancients.**
   a. Cultural Offerings of the Ancient East.
     i. The dawn and rise of civilizations.
     ii. Means of transmission of culture.
   b. Lasting Effects of Greek Life.
     i. Peculiar accomplishments of the Greeks.
     ii. Dissemination of culture in the Hellenistic **Age**.
     iii. Evolution of occidental types of culture.

3. **The Barbarian Migrations: Social Fluidity**
   c. Influences of Roman Civilization.
      i. Rise of the Roman state: economic foundations.
      ii. Mingling of East and West in the Roman Empire.
      iii. Development of unique political institutions.
      iv. The permanence of Roman influence.
      v. Means of transmission of Roman culture.

   Turner, *Europe, 1450-1789*, pp. 28, 58-9, 274-275.

   Parallel References:
   ADAMS, *Civilization During the Middle Ages*, ch. 2.
   BRYCE, *The Holy Roman Empire*, ch. 2.
   EMERTON, *Introduction to the Middle Ages*, ch. 1.
   MUNRO, *The Middle Ages*, ch. 1.
   MUNRO AND SELLERY, *Medieval Civilization*, pp. 3-43.
   ROBINSON, *History of Western Europe*, I, pp. 17-27.
   ROBINSON, *Introduction to the History of Western Europe*, pp. 8-24.
   STILLÉ, *Studies in Medieval History*, pp. 13-20.
   THATCHER AND McNEAL, *Europe in the Middle Age*, ch. 1.

   Supplementary References:
   (A review of any good ancient history is recommended. Special reference to the following books is suggested.) BURY, *History of the Later Roman Empire*, vol. I; CROCE, *History: Its Theory and Practice*, pt. II; CUNNINGHAM, *Western Civilization*, ch. I; FERRERO, *The Ruin of Ancient Civilization and the Triumph of Christianity*, chs. 1-3; GIBBON, *Decline and Fall of the Roman Empire*, passim; *History of All Nations*, vols. I, III, IV; SHOTWELL, *An Introduction to the History of History*, chs. 5-7, *passim*.

B. **DECLINE OF CLASSICAL CIVILIZATION.**

3. **The Barbarian Migrations: Social Fluidity.**
   a. Origin and Nature of the Invaders.
      i. Races represented: their institutions.
      ii. Causes and nature of barbarian movements.
   b. Routes of Progress: Significance.
   c. End of the Roman Empire in the West.
      i. Flooding of the Roman provinces.
      ii. Character of the "fall" of Rome.
      iii. Location of barbarian groups.
      iv. Foundations of a new political order.
         (a) Rise of barbarian kingdoms.
         (b) Embryos of modern political entities.

4. **Guiding Influences of the Christian Church**
   d. Coming of the Dark Ages.
      i. The submerging of Roman culture.
      ii. Return to primitive institutions.
      iii. Continuity provided by the Christian Church.

   Turner, *Europe, 1450-1789*, pp. 242-3, 315, 317, *passim*.

   Parallel References:
   BRYCE, *The Holy Roman Empire*, ch. 3.
   DAVIS, *Medieval Europe*, pp. 12-40.
   EMERTON, *Introduction to the Middle Ages*, pp. 11-48.
   MUNRO, *The Middle Ages*, chs. 3-5.
   MUNRO AND SELLERY, *Medieval Civilization*, pp. 44-86.
   ROBINSON, *History of Western Europe*, I, pp. 39-55.
   ROBINSON, *Introduction to the History of Western Europe*, pp. 25-43.
   SEIGNOBOS, *History of Mediæval and Modern Civilization*, ch. 1.
   STILLÉ, *Studies in Medieval History*, pp. 20-26, 41-53.
   THATCHER AND McNEAL, *Europe in the Middle Age*, ch. 2.
   THORNDIKE, *History of Mediæval Europe*, ch. 5.

   Supplementary References:
   ADAMS, *Civilization During the Middle Ages*, ch. 4; *Cambridge Mediæval History*, I, chs. 7, 9-11, 14, 15; II, chs. 4-8; GRANT, *Passing of the Great Race*, pp. 99-100, 156 ff., 179-187; HENDERSON, *A Short History of Germany*, I, ch. 1; *History of All Nations*, VI, chs. 9-15, 19-22; MORRIS, *Beginnings of the Middle Ages*, pp. 6-30; OMAN, *The Dark Ages*, pp. 1-32, 76-88, 96-106, *passim*; WHITMAN, *Austria*, chs. 2-3.

   Source Readings:
   OGG, *Source Book of Mediæval History*, chs. 1-3; ROBINSON, *Readings in European History*, I, pp. 28-34; THATCHER AND McNEAL, *Source Book for Mediæval History*, pp. 2-11.

4. **Guiding Influences of the Christian Church.**
   a. Conditions Favoring a New Religion.
      i. Pantheistic tendencies in the Empire.
      ii. The peculiar appeal of the new faith.
      iii. Discrediting of older creeds and philosophies.
   b. Spread of the Christian Faith.
      i. Methods of propagation: the Church at Antioch.
      ii. Missionary endeavors: westward migration.

5. The Challenge of Islam to the Western World

  c. Beginnings of Church Organization.
    i. Nature of early Christian groups.
    ii. The rise of elders and patriarchs.
    iii. Effects of persecution: the Christian martyrs.
    iv. Features of Early Church culture: the Bible.
  d. Foundations of the Papal Office.
    i. The confusion of Christian tongues: Nicæa.
    ii. The Roman Bishop as heir of the Emperor.
    iii. Proselyting activities of the Roman Church.
    iv. Traditions of Rome: extinction of rival churches.

Turner, *Europe, 1450-1789*, pp. 23-30.

Parallel References:
Bémont and Monod, *Medieval Europe*, pp. 15-18, 119-124.
Bryce, *The Holy Roman Empire*, pp. 9-14.
Davis, *Medieval Europe*, pp. 109-114.
Emerton, *Introduction to the Middle Ages*, pp. 92-114.
Munro, *The Middle Ages*, chs. 2, 6.
Robinson, *History of Western Europe*, I, pp. 27-38, 56-83.
Robinson, *Introduction to the History of Western Europe*, pp. 44-66.
Seignobos, *History of Mediæval and Modern Civilization*, ch. 2.
Stillé, *Studies in Medieval History*, pp. 26-35, 53-58.
Swinton, *Outlines of History*, sec. IV, ch. 5.
Thatcher and McNeal, *Europe in the Middle Age*, ch. 8.
Thorndike, *History of Medieval Europe*, chs. 6, 9.

Supplementary References:
Adams, *Civilization During the Middle Ages*, ch. 3; *Cambridge Mediæval History*, I, chs. 4-6; II, chs. 8, 22; Ferrero, *Ruin of Ancient Civilization and Triumph of Christianity*, ch. 4; Morris, *Beginnings of the Middle Ages*, pp. 47-53; Oman, *The Dark Ages*, pp. 272-281; Taylor, *The Classical Heritage of the Middle Ages*, ch. 2; Taylor, *The Mediæval Mind*, I, chs. 1-6.

Source Readings:
Ogg, *Source Book of Mediæval History*, pp. 78-97; Robinson, *Readings in European History*, I, pp. 18-28, 63-82; Thatcher and McNeal, *Source Book for Mediæval History*, pp. 82-93.

5. The Challenge of Islam to the Western World.
  a. The Rise of Islam.
    i. Mohammed and his religion: the Koran.
    ii. The static phase: the *Hegira*.
    iii. The aggressive phase: the faith militant.

6. **The Carolingian Empire: Crystallizing Processes**
   b. Spreading of the Faith by the Sword.
      i. Asiatic expansion: organization of conquests.
      ii. Points of attack on Christian Europe.
         (a) Contact with the Eastern Roman Empire.
         (b) A century of progress toward Christian Spain.
      iii. The Moors in Spain and France: Tours.
   c. The Influence of Arabian Culture.
      i. Spain as a center of civilization.
         (a) Features of Mohammedan culture.
         (b) Leavening effect on western Europe.
      ii. The Christian recovery of Spain.
      iii. Partial disruption of the Mohammedan world.

   Turner, *Europe 1450-1789*, pp. 314-318, 67 ff.

   Parallel References:
   BÉMONT AND MONOD, *Medieval Europe*, chs. 10, 11.
   EMERTON, *Introduction to the Middle Ages*, pp. 122-128.
   MUNRO, *The Middle Ages*, chs. 11, 19.
   ROBINSON, *History of Western Europe*, I, pp. 84-96.
   ROBINSON, *Introduction to the History of Western Europe*, pp. 68-72.
   SEIGNOBOS, *History of Mediæval and Modern Civilization*, ch. 4.
   STILLÉ, *Studies in Medieval History*, ch. 4.
   SWINTON, *Outlines of History*, sec. IV, ch. 2.
   THATCHER AND MCNEAL, *Europe in the Middle Age*, ch. 14.
   THORNDIKE, *History of Medieval Europe*, ch. 10.

   Supplementary References:
   Cambridge Mediæval History, II, chs. 10-12; DAVIS, *A Short History of the Near East*, chs. 9-14; *History of All Nations*, VII, ch. 6; LANE-POOLE, *The Moors in Spain;* MERRIMAN, *The Rise of the Spanish Empire*, I, pp. 13-25, 53-91; MORRIS, *Beginnings of the Middle Ages*, ch. 6; MUNRO AND SELLERY, *Medieval Civilization*, pp. 224-240; OMAN, *The Story of the Byzantine Empire*, ch. 12; SCHEVILL, *The History of the Balkan Peninsula*, chs. 6, 12-13.

   Source Readings:
   OGG, *Source Book of Mediæval History*, ch. 7; ROBINSON, *Readings in European History*, I, pp. 116-120.

6. **The Carolingian Empire: Crystallizing Processes.**
   a. Rise of the Frankish Kingdom.
      i. Growth of the Merovingian domain.
      ii. Accession of the Carolingians: Charles Martel.
      iii. The Alliance with the Papacy.

6. The Carolingian Empire: Crystallizing Processes

b. Conquest and Empire.
  i. Campaigns of Charlemagne.
  ii. The Lombards and the temporal power of the Papacy.
  iii. Creation of the Empire: significance.
  iv. Degree of unity of western Europe.
c. Influences of the Empire of Charlemagne.
  i. Unique features of Carolingian government.
    (a) Democratic elements: the "May Field."
    (b) *Missi* and *dominici*.
  ii. The "Carolingian Renaissance."
  iii. Relation of Church and State: a tradition.

Turner, *Europe, 1450-1789*, pp. 49-50, 242-244, *passim*.

Parallel References:
ADAMS, *Civilization During the Middle Ages*, pp. 151-165.
BÉMONT AND MONOD, *Medieval Europe*, pp. 179-211.
DAVIS, *Medieval Europe*, pp. 40-67.
ROBINSON, *History of Western Europe*, I, pp. 97-117.
ROBINSON, *Introduction to the History of Western Europe*, pp. 34-38, 67-8, 72-91.
SEIGNOBOS, *History of Mediæval and Modern Civilization*, ch. 5.
STILLÉ, *Studies in Medieval History*, pp. 58-97.
SWINTON, *Outlines of History*, sec. IV, ch. 3.
THATCHER AND MCNEAL, *Europe in the Middle Age*, ch. 5.
THORNDIKE, *History of Medieval Europe*, ch. 11.

Supplementary References:
BRYCE, *The Holy Roman Empire*, chs. 4-5; *Cambridge Mediæval History*, II, chs. 18-21; III, chs. 1-3; EINHARD, *Life of Charlemagne*; HENDERSON, *Germany in the Middle Ages*, pp. 46-116, 150-235; *History of All Nations*, VII, ch. 2; VIII, chs. 1-5; HODGKIN, *Italy and Her Invaders*, *passim*; MORRIS, *Beginnings of the Middle Ages*, ch. 5; MUNRO, *The Middle Ages*, chs. 7-8, 10-11; TAYLOR, *The Mediæval Mind*, I, ch. 10; OMAN, *The Dark Ages*, chs. 20-22; SERGEANT, *The Franks*, chs. 1-15.

Source Readings:
HENDERSON, *Historical Documents of the Middle Ages*, pp. 170-172, 199-207; OGG, *Source Book of Mediæval History*, pp. 105-108; ROBINSON, *Readings in European History*, I, p. 12; THATCHER AND MCNEAL, *Source Book for Mediæval History*, pp. 37-38, 55-59; UNIVERSITY OF PENNSYLVANIA, *Translations and Reprints*, VI, no. 5; III, no. 2.

7. The Evolution of the Feudal Order

II. MEDIEVAL DEVELOPMENT

A. THE REMOLDING OF EUROPE.
7. The Evolution of the Feudal Order.
   a. The Disruption of the Carolingian Empire.
      i. Beginning of a new era of wars.
      ii. The Treaties of Verdun and Mersen.
         (a) Lines of political cleavage: buffer states.
         (b) Relation to future national boundaries.
      iii. Decay of the Carolingians.
      iv. Formation of new Germanic Kingdoms.
   b. The Development of a Feudal Order.
      i. Feudalism as an emergency measure.
         (a) Bases of feudal life: service and protection.
         (b) Character of feudal relationships.
      ii. Variations in feudal theory and practice.
      iii. The feudalizing of all institutions.
      iv. Limitations of feudal culture: chivalry.

Turner, *Europe, 1450-1789*, pp. 3-19, *passim.*

Parallel References:
BÉMONT AND MONOD, *Medieval Europe*, ch. 14.
DAVIS, *Medieval Europe*, pp. 67-68, 87-108.
EMERTON, *Introduction to the Middle Ages*, pp. 236-255.
EMERTON, *Mediæval Europe*, pp. 90-115.
ROBINSON, *History of Western Europe*, I, pp. 117-139.
ROBINSON, *Introduction to the History of Western Europe*, pp. 92-119.
SEIGNOBOS. *History of Mediæval and Modern Civilization*, ch. 6.
STILLÉ, *Studies in Medieval History*, pp. 95-98, 127-145.
SWINTON, *Outlines of History*, sec. IV, ch. 4.
THATCHER AND MCNEAL, *Europe in the Middle Age*, chs. 6-7.
THORNDIKE, *History of Medieval Europe*, chs. 12-13.

Supplementary References:
ADAMS, *Civilization During the Middle Ages*, pp. 170-227; BRYCE, *The Holy Roman Empire*, ch. 6; *Cambridge Mediæval History*, III, ch. 4; CUTTS, *Scenes and Characters of the Middle Ages*, pp. 311-460; FUNCK-BRENTANO, *The Middle Ages*, chs. 1-2; *History of All Nations*, VIII, ch. 6; MORRIS, *Beginnings of the Middle Ages*, pp. 147-175; OMAN, *The Dark Ages*, chs. 23-28.

8. Creation of the French Monarchy

Source Readings:
HENDERSON, *Historical Documents of the Middle Ages*, pp. 172, 173, 208–215; OGG, *Source Book of Mediæval History*, pp. 149–177, 203–233; ROBINSON, *Readings in European History*, I, pp. 150–158, 175–195; THATCHER AND MCNEAL, *Source Book for Mediæval History*, pp. 59–65, 341–387, 363–368; UNIVERSITY OF PENNSYLVANIA, *Translations and Reprints*, IV, no. 3.

8. Creation of the French Monarchy.
   a. The Feudal Origin of France.
      i. Decline of the Carolingians in the West.
      ii. Accession of the Capetians: their ability.
      iii. Gradual centralization of French institutions.
   b. Steps in the Consolidation of France.
      i. Results of the Norman conquest of England.
      ii. Reduction of competitive feudal states.
         (a) Philip II and the seizure of the Angevin lands.
         (b) Aggressiveness of Philip IV and Louis XI.
      iii. French participation in the Crusades.
      iv. Calling of the first Estates General.
   c. The Accession of the Valois Line.
      i. Progress of French institutions and culture.
      ii. Close connection and rivalry of France and England.
      iii. Lack of natural French boundaries.
      iv. France at the time of the Bourbon accession.

Turner, *Europe, 1450-1789*, pp. 356-374, ff.

Parallel References:
BÉMONT AND MONOD, *Medieval Europe*, chs. 24–26.
DAVIS, *Medieval Europe*, ch. 7, *passim*.
EMERTON, *Mediæval Europe*, pp. 400–433.
ROBINSON, *History of Western Europe*, I, pp. 140–145, 158–162.
ROBINSON, *Introduction to the History of Western Europe*, pp. 120–132.
SEIGNOBOS, *History of Mediæval and Modern Civilization*, pp. 120–125, 173–178.
STILLÉ, *Studies in Medieval History*, pp. 145–157.
THATCHER AND MCNEAL, *Europe in the Middle Age*, ch. 16.
THORNDIKE, *History of Medieval Europe*, pp. 266–273, 490–510.

9. Rise of the English Kingdom

Supplementary References:
ADAMS, *Growth of the French Nation*, pp. 54–78; *Cambridge Mediæval History*, III, chs. 4–5; FUNCK-BRENTANO, *The Middle Ages*, chs. 4, 6–15; *History of All Nations*, IX, chs. 5, 12, 18; LODGE, *Close of the Middle Ages*, chs. 2–3; MASSON, *Mediæval France*, pp. 13–21, 47–158; MUNRO, *The Middle Ages*, chs. 16, 23; TOUT, *Empire and Papacy*, pp. 66–95, 274–294, 393–427.

Source Readings:
OGG, *Source Book of Mediæval History*, pp. 311–324; ROBINSON, *Readings in European History*, I, pp. 194–221; THATCHER AND MCNEAL, *Source Book for Mediæval History*, p. 227.

9. **Rise of the English Kingdom.**
   a. Anglo-Saxon England.
      i. Origins of the English: successive conquests.
      ii. Political development: local political institutions.
      iii. Provincialism of Anglo-Saxon England.
   b. Effects of the Norman Conquest.
      i. Background of the conquest: William of Normandy.
      ii. Character of the invasion: Hastings.
      iii. Disposition of the conquered realm: Norman rule.
      iv. Cultural effects of the conquest.
   c. Beginnings of the English Nation.
      i. Gradual rise of an English people and language.
      ii. Centralization of government under the Normans.
      iii. Foundation of the constitution: Magna Charta.
   d. The Origins of Parliament.
      i. Merging of Norman and Saxon institutions.
      ii. The "Model Parliament" of Edward I.
      iii. Effects of the Wars of the Roses.
      iv. Relations with Wales, Ireland, and Scotland.

Turner, *Europe, 1450-1789*, pp. 411-416.

Parallel References:
ADAMS, *Civilization During the Middle Ages*, pp. 332–355.
BÉMONT AND MONOD, *Medieval Europe*, pp. 124–134, 189, 445–466.
DAVIS, *Medieval Europe*, pp. 153–160, *passim*.
ROBINSON, *History of Western Europe*, I, pp. 146–158, 163–170.
ROBINSON, *Introduction to the History of Western Europe*, pp. 133–147.

10. The Holy Roman Empire: the Universal State

SEIGNOBOS, *History of Mediæval and Modern Civilization*, pp. 152–159.
STILLÉ, *Studies in Medieval History*, chs. 7–8.
SWINTON, *Outlines of History*, sec. IV, ch. 2.
THATCHER AND MCNEAL, *Europe in the Middle Age*, chs. 17–18.
THORNDIKE, *History of Medieval Europe*, pp. 219–223, 275–279, 295–298, 456–460, 474–489.

Supplementary References:
Cambridge Mediæval History, I, ch. 13; II, ch. 17; III, chs. 14–15; *Cambridge Modern History*, I, ch. 14; CHEYNEY, *Industrial and Social History of England*, pp. 1–28; CHEYNEY, *Short History of England*, chs. 1–9; CROSS, *A History of England and Greater Britain*, chs. 1–18; GREEN, *Short History of the English People*, pp. 3–71, *ff. History of All Nations*, VII, ch. 3; IX, chs. 5, 12, 18; X, ch. 14; LARSON, *History of England and the British Commonwealth*, chs. 1–9; MUNRO, *The Middle Ages*, chs. 17–18, 22; OGG, *Governments of Europe*, ch. 1.

Source Readings:
CHEYNEY, *Readings in English History*, chs. 4–9; HENDERSON, *Historical Documents of the Middle Ages*, pp. 1–20, 135–165; OGG, *Source Book of Mediæval History*, pp. 297–310; ROBINSON, *Readings in European History*, I, pp. 221–244; THATCHER AND MCNEAL, *Source Book for Mediæval History*, pp. 219, 228; UNIVERSITY OF PENNSYLVANIA, *Translations and Reprints*, I, no. 6; II, no. 1.

10. The Holy Roman Empire: the Universal State.

a. Theories of the Relation of Church and State.
   i. Papal re-creation of the Empire: 800 A. D.
   ii. Lapse of the imperial title.
   iii. Revival of the Empire by Otto I.
      (a) Services of Otto to the Papal Office.
      (b) Future identification of the Empire with Germany.

b. Struggles of State and Church for Supremacy.
   i. The Investiture Conflict.
      (a) Political influence of the clergy: lay investiture.
      (b) The inevitable clash of spiritual and temporal sovereigns.
   ii. Incidents in the struggle for power.
      (a) The duel of Gregory VII and Henry IV: Canossa.

11. Organization and Functions of the Universal Church

        (b) Papal clashes with French and English Kings.
- iii. The Concordat of Worms: importance.
- iv. Later phases of the issue in Germany.
- c. Importance of the Holy Roman Empire.
  - i. Disorganization of Germany and Italy.
  - ii. Deleterious influences in Church administration.

Turner, *Europe, 1450-1789*, pp. 50-51, 65, 242-248, *passim*.

Parallel References:
ADAMS, *Civilization During the Middle Ages*, chs. 4, 10.
BÉMONT AND MONOD, *Medieval Europe*, chs. 16-20.
DAVIS, *Medieval Europe*, pp. 68-86, 114-152.
EMERTON, *Mediæval Europe*, pp. 89-114, 235-332.
ROBINSON, *History of Western Europe*, I, pp. 179-231.
ROBINSON, *Introduction to the History of Western Europe*, pp. 148-186.
STILLÉ, *Studies in Medieval History*, pp. 277-299.
THATCHER AND MCNEAL, *Europe in the Middle Age*, chs. 10-13.
THORNDIKE, *History of Medieval Europe*, pp. 256-265, 203-206.

Supplementary References:
BRYCE, *The Holy Roman Empire*, pp. 89-120, 132-139, 153-183, 204-229; *Cambridge Mediæval History*, III, chs. 7-8, 17; HENDERSON, *Germany in the Middle Ages*, pp. 112-179, 182-409; *History of All Nations*, VIII, chs. 10-11; IX, chs. 1-4; X, ch. 12; LODGE, *The Close of the Middle Ages*, chs. 1-2; MUNRO, *The Middle Ages*, chs. 14-15; OMAN, *The Dark Ages*, pp. 468-477; TOUT, *Empire and Papacy*, pp. 12-62, 120-150, 221-273, 304-392.

Source Readings:
HENDERSON, *Historical Documents of the Middle Ages*, pp. 351-432; OGG, *Source Book of Mediæval History*, pp. 261-281; ROBINSON, *Readings in European History*, I, pp. 245-256, 296-311; THATCHER AND MCNEAL, *Source Book for Mediæval History*, pp. 115-126.

B. THE CLIMAX OF MEDIEVAL LIFE AND CULTURE.

11. Organization and Functions of the Universal Church.
- a. The Feudalization of the Church.
  - i. Extent of Church property: sources of income.
  - ii. Feudal control of Church lands.

11. Organization and Functions of the Universal Church
- b. Organization of the Catholic Church.
  - i. The secular branch of the Church: functions.
  - ii. Origin and duties of the regular clergy.
    - (a) Rise of monasticism.
    - (b) Religious revivals: Cluny.
  - iii. Rise of mendicant and fraternal orders.
  - iv. Social functions of monastic establishments.
    - (a) Monasteries as public service institutions.
    - (b) Preservation of learning: centers of culture.
- c. Powers and Duties of the Church.
  - i. Papal authority: position of Church Councils.
  - ii. Definition of heresy: Albigenses and Waldenses.
  - iii. Methods of extirpating heresy.

Turner, *Europe, 1450-1789*, pp. 23-34, 697.

Parallel References:
ADAMS, *Civilization During the Middle Ages*, ch. 16.
BÉMONT AND MONOD, *Medieval Europe*, chs. 29-30.
EMERTON, *Mediæval Europe*, pp. 49-53, 333-338, 541-555.
ROBINSON, *History of Western Europe*, I, pp. 226-259.
ROBINSON, *Introduction to the History of Western Europe*, pp. 201-232.
SCHEVILL, *Political History of Modern Europe*, ch. 3.
SEIGNOBOS, *History of Medieval and Modern Civilization*, ch. 7.
STILLÉ, *Studies in Medieval History*, ch. 9, pp. 298-304.
THATCHER AND MCNEAL, *Europe in the Middle Age*, pp. 165-181, 403-413.
THORNDIKE, *History of Medieval Europe*, pp. 434-454, 560-575.

Supplementary References:
BARRY, *The Papal Monarchy; Cambridge Modern History*, I, chs. 17-19; CUTTS, *Scenes and Characters of the Middle Ages*, pp. 1-56, 195-265; *History of All Nations*, X, ch. 7; LEA, *History of the Inquisition*, I, *passim*; LODGE, *The Close of the Middle Ages*, chs. 5-11; MUNRO, *The Middle Ages*, pp. 83-85, 237, 381-383, chs. 27, 30; MUNRO AND SELLERY, *Medieval Civilization*, pp. 129-158, 188-209; SOHM, *Outlines of Church History*, pp. 66-73, 116-145; TAYLOR, *The Mediæval Mind*, I, chs. 11-24.

Source Readings:
OGG, *Source Book of Mediæval History*, pp. 362-397; ROBINSON, *Readings in European History*, I, pp. 346-387; THATCHER AND

12. The Crusades: Composite Enterprises

McNeal, *Source Book for Mediæval History*, pp. 432-509; University of Pennsylvania, *Translations and Reprints*, III, no. 6, pp. 6-25.

12. The Crusades: Composite Enterprises.
    a. Forces Producing the Crusades.
        i. Restlessness and zeal of western peoples.
        ii. Plight of the Byzantine Empire.
        iii. The religious appeal: Clermont.
        iv. Minor contributing factors: feudal conditions.
    b. Character of the Crusades in the East.
        i. Forming of irregular armies: their composition.
        ii. The Crusades as migrations.
        iii. Conquest and organization of eastern lands.
        iv. Degeneration of later crusades.
    c. Crusading Movements in Europe.
        i. Motives operating in local movements.
        ii. Expeditions to Spain and Prussia: minor undertakings.
    d. Results and Significance of the Enterprises.
        i. Economic effects: the Fourth Crusade.
        ii. Widening of the European horizon.
        iii. Bearing on the development of western culture.

Turner, *Europe, 1450-1789,* pp. 19, 40-42, 66-67, 299.

Parallel References:
Adams, *Civilization during the Middle Ages,* ch. 11.
Bémont and Monod, *Medieval Europe,* ch. 12.
Davis, *Medieval Europe,* ch. 8.
Emerton, *Mediæval Europe,* pp. 358-397.
Robinson, *History of Western Europe,* I, pp. 214-225.
Robinson, *Introduction to the History of Western Europe,* pp. 182-200.
Seignobos, *History of Mediæval and Modern Civilization,* ch. 8.
Stillé, *Studies in Medieval History,* pp. 353-358, 427-428.
Swinton, *Outlines of History,* sec. IV, ch. 6.
Thatcher and McNeal, *Europe in the Middle Age,* ch. 15.
Thorndike, *History of Medieval Europe,* pp. 310-325.

13. Prevailing Economic and Social Conditions

Supplementary References:
ARCHER AND KINGSFORD, *The Crusades; Cambridge Mediæval History*, IV, chs. 13–15; *Cambridge Modern History*, I, ch. 8; COX, *The Crusades*; FUNCK-BRENTANO, *The Middle Ages*, ch. 5; *History of All Nations*, IX, chs. 6, 13, 14; MOMBERT, *Short History of the Crusades;* MUNRO, *The Middle Ages*, chs. 21, 25; MUNRO AND SELLERY, *Medieval Civilization*, pp. 248–276; TOUT, *Empire and Papacy*, pp. 167–197, 295–304, 342–357, 450–463; WEBSTER, *General History of Commerce*, ch. 8.

Source Readings:
HENDERSON, *Historical Documents of the Middle Ages*, pp. 135, 333–344; OGG, *Source Book of Mediæval History*, pp. 282–296; ROBINSON, *Readings in European History*, I, pp. 329–343; THATCHER AND MCNEAL, *Source Book for Mediæval History*, pp. 510–544; UNIVERSITY OF PENNSYLVANIA, *Translations and Reprints*, I, nos. 2, 4; III, no. 1.

13. Prevailing Economic and Social Conditions.
a. Styles of Domestic Life.
  i. Medieval social strata: feudal basis.
  ii. Habits and activities of the nobility: the castle.
  iii. Contrasting wretchedness of the peasantry.
b. The Rise of Towns and Gilds.
  i. Causes of the revival of urban life.
  ii. Characteristic features of towns and cities.
    (a) Diversity of occupations.
    (b) Securing of political privilege and exemption.
  iii. The place of towns in cultural development.
    (a) The town as the center of wealth.
    (b) Patronage of the arts: group activities.
c. Medieval Industry.
  i. The relation of industry and trade.
  ii. Rise of trades unions.
    (a) Types of merchant gilds.
    (b) Trade gilds: uniformity and monopoly.
    (c) Comparison with modern organizations.

Turner, *Europe, 1450-1789*, pp. 19-23.

Parallel References:
BÉMONT AND MONOD, *Medieval Europe*, pp. 375–387.
EMERTON, *Beginnings of Modern Europe*, pp. 239–241.
HAYES, *Political and Social History of Modern Europe*, I, pp. 28–43.

14. Medieval Learning and Philosophy

Robinson, *History of Western Europe*, I, pp. 260–270.
Robinson, *Introduction to the History of Western Europe*, pp. 233–249.
Schevill, *Political History of Modern Europe*, pp. 21–24.
Stillé, *Studies in Medieval History*, pp. 313–331, 390–407.
Swinton, *Outlines of the World's History*, sec. IV, pp. 276–280.
Thatcher and McNeal, *Europe in the Middle Age*, pp. 435–445.
Thorndike, *History of Medieval Europe*, pp. 232–253, 327–340.

Supplementary References:
Cambridge Modern History, I, ch. 15; Cheyney, *Industrial and Social History of England*, chs. 2–4; Cunningham, *Western Civilization in Its Economic Aspects*, II, pp. 54–62, 89–106; Cutts, *Scenes and Characters of the Middle Ages*, pp. 518–546; Emerton, *Mediæval Europe*, ch. 15; Funck-Brentano, *The Middle Ages*, ch. 16; Munro, *The Middle Ages*, chs. 26, 28; Ogg, *Economic Development of Modern Europe*, chs. 1–3; Seignobos, *History of Mediæval and Modern Civilization*, pp. 140–146, 192–204.

Source Readings:
Robinson, *Readings in European History*, I, pp. 399–412; Thatcher and McNeal, *Source Book for Mediæval History*, pp. 549–551, 604–612; University of Pennsylvania, *Translations and Reprints*, II, no. 1; III, no. 5.

14. **Medieval Learning and Philosophy.**
   a. The Character of Medieval Education.
      i. The intellectual status of the Middle Ages.
      ii. Church control of education.
         (a) The Church as keeper of records and as school.
         (b) Character of religious instruction.
      iii. Origin and rise of universities.
         (a) Origin of instruction gilds: Church influence.
         (b) Noted medieval institutions: curricula.
      iv. Influence of Byzantine and Mohammedan culture.
   b. Scholasticism and the Schoolmen.
      i. Relation of Scholasticism to the universities.
      ii. Exponents of the Scholastic movement: Abelard.
      iii. Elements of medieval science: Roger Bacon.

15. **The Italian Background of the Renaissance**
    iv. Connection of science and philosophy: logic.
    v. Relation of Scholasticism to the Renaissance.

Turner, *Europe, 1450-1789*, pp. 101-112, ch. 24, *passim*.

Parallel References:
ADAMS, *Civilization During the Middle Ages*, pp. 365-373.
BÉMONT AND MONOD, *Medieval Europe*, ch. 31.
HAYES, *Political and Social History of Modern Europe*, I, pp. 175-177.
ROBINSON, *History of Western Europe*, I, pp. 290-309.
ROBINSON, *Introduction to the History of Western Europe*, pp. 267-276.
SEIGNOBOS, *History of Mediæval and Modern Civilization*, pp. 125-132.
STILLÉ, *Studies in Medieval History*, ch. 13.
SWINTON, *Outlines of History*, sec. IV, pp. 280-284.
THATCHER AND MCNEAL, *Europe in the Middle Age*, pp. 456-495.
THORNDIKE, *History of Medieval Europe*, pp. 373-432.

Supplementary References:
ABBOTT, *Expansion of Europe*, I, ch. 1; EMERTON, *Mediæval Europe*, pp. 446-476; FUNCK-BRENTANO, *The Middle Ages*, ch. 3; HASKINS, *The Rise of Universities*; HASKINS, *Studies in the History of Mediæval Science*; *History of All Nations*, X, ch. 7; MUNRO, *The Middle Ages*, ch. 31; TAYLOR, *The Mediæval Mind*, II, chs. 25-44; TOUT, *Empire and Papacy*, pp. 209-220, 428-432, 446-449.

Source Readings:
OGG, *Source Book of Mediæval History*, pp. 340-361; ROBINSON, *Readings in European History*, I, pp. 446-461; UNIVERSITY OF PENNSYLVANIA, *Translations and Reprints*, II, no. 3.

III. THE ERA OF THE RENAISSANCE

A. THE EXPANDING OF HUMAN INTERESTS.

15. **The Italian Background of the Renaissance.**
    a. The Political Situation in Italy.
        i. Disunity: the Holy Roman Empire.
        ii. Italian city-states as guardians of liberty.
            (a) City leagues and inter-state wars.
            (b) Struggles with German, French and Spanish kings.

15. The Italian Background of the Renaissance

b. The *Rationale* of the Italian Renaissance.
  i. The relation of commerce, towns and culture.
  ii. Remains of ancient civilization in Italy.
  iii. Effects of the fall of the Byzantine Empire.
  iv. The New Learning: Italian exponents.
c. Characteristics of the Reawakening.
  i. Services of the Humanists: the classics.
  ii. Progress in the fine arts: literature.
d. Spread of the Renaissance.
  i. Rise of a critical, questioning spirit.
  ii. Evidences of the scientific attitude.
  iii. Northward progress of the movement.

Turner, *Europe, 1450-1789*, pp. 112-118, 122-127.

Parallel References:
ADAMS, *Civilization During the Middle Ages*, pp. 356-375.
EMERTON, *Beginnings of Modern Europe*, ch. 9.
HAYES, *Political and Social History of Modern Europe*, I, pp. 177-185.
ROBINSON, *History of Western Europe*, I, pp. 310-335.
ROBINSON, *Introduction to the History of Western Europe*, pp. 321-353.
SCHEVILL, *Political History of Modern Europe*, pp. 15-18, 59-65.
SEIGNOBOS, *History of Mediæval and Modern Civilization*, pp. 132-139, ch. 17.
THATCHER AND MCNEAL, *Europe in the Middle Age*, pp. 496-502.
THORNDIKE, *History of Medieval Europe*, pp. 576-593.

Supplementary References:
ABBOTT, *Expansion of Europe*, I, pp. 43-48; BRYCE, *Holy Roman Empire*, ch. 18; *Cambridge Modern History*, I, ch. 16; HALLAM, *The Middle Ages*, pt. II, pp. 179-235; *History of All Nations*, X, ch. 16; XI, ch. 7; HULME, *Renaissance and Reformation*, pp. 50-124; LODGE, *The Close of the Middle Ages*, ch. 22; MUNRO, *The Middle Ages*, ch. 20; TANNER, *The Renaissance and the Reformation*, ch. 1.

Source Readings:
OGG, *Source Book of Mediæval History*, pp. 445-473; ROBINSON, *Readings in European History*, I, pp. 520-531; WHITCOMB, *A Literary Source-Book of the Italian Renaissance*.

16. Culture of the Renaissance Era

16. Culture of the Renaissance Era.
   a. The Development of Vernacular Literature.
      i. Evolution of the Western European languages.
      ii. Subject matter of Renaissance works.
         (a) Secular literature: emancipation of literary art.
         (b) Early examples of vernacular writings.
   b. Renaissance Spirit in Art and Architecture.
      i. Evidences of the New Learning in art.
         (a) Leading exponents of schools of art: painting.
         (b) The rapid production of great masterpieces.
         (c) The trend toward modernism.
      ii. Origin of architectural styles.
         (a) Application of the Gothic type.
         (b) Oriental influences: regard for the Byzantine.
      iii. Architectural expression in Church edifices.
      iv. Typical examples of Renaissance structures.
   c. Cultural Effects of the New Movement.
      i. The escape from tradition: original thought.
      ii. Stimulating effects on all human activities.

Turner, *Europe, 1450-1789*, pp. 124-126, 794-819, ch. 25, *passim*.

Parallel References:
ADAMS, *Civilization During the Middle Ages*, pp. 375-382.
EMERTON, *Beginnings of Modern Europe*, ch. 10.
HAYES, *Political and Social History of Modern Europe*, I, pp. 185-201.
ROBINSON, *History of Western Europe*, I, pp. 335-352.
ROBINSON, *Introduction to the History of Western Europe*, pp. 250-267, 339-346.
SCHEVILL, *Political History of Modern Europe*, pp. 19-24.
SWINTON, *Outlines of the World's History*, sec. V, pp. 312-314.
THATCHER AND MCNEAL, *Europe in the Middle Age*, pp. 502-508.
THORNDIKE, *History of Medieval Europe*, pp. 593-612.

Supplementary References:
ABBOTT, *Expansion of Europe*, I, pp. 48-64; BRYCE, *Holy Roman Empire*, ch. 15; *Cambridge Modern History*, I, chs. 1-2; FISKE, *The Discovery of America*, I, chs. 2-6; *History of All*

17. The Widening of European Horizons

Nations, XI, chs. 7, 16; HULME, *Renaissance and Reformation*, pp. 124–188; LODGE, *Close of the Middle Ages*, pp. 490–495; SEIGNOBOS, *History of Mediæval and Modern Civilization*, ch. 19; SYMONDS, *Short History of the Renaissance in Italy*, ch. 12; TANNER, *The Renaissance and the Reformation*, ch. 2; WEBSTER, *General History of Commerce*, chs. 8, 14.

Source Readings:
ROBINSON, *Readings in European History*, I, pp. 531–541.

17. **The Widening of European Horizons.**
    a. The Revival of Trade in Medieval Times.
        i. Influences of the Crusades.
        ii. The development of trade with the East.
            (a) The Mediterranean as a commerical waterway.
            (b) Trade routes from the Levant eastward.
        iii. Lines of trade in Europe.
            (a) The extensive use of waterways.
            (b) Principal overland highways.
    b. Rise of Commercial Organizations.
        i. The handicaps and attractions of trade.
        ii. Trade organizations and monopolies: Hanseatic League.
        iii. Distribution through fairs and markets: location.
    c. Growth of Geographical Knowledge: Age of Discovery.
        i. Improvements in ship building and navigation.
        ii. Exploits in discovery and exploration.
        iii. Mental escape from local environment: the printing press.

Turner, *Europe, 1450-1789*, pp. 118-122, 129-148.

Parallel References:
ADAMS, *Civilization During the Middle Ages*, ch. 12.
BÉMONT AND MONOD, *Medieval Europe*, pp. 386–390, 483, 513.
HAYES, *Political and Social History of Modern Europe*, I, pp. 43–49.
ROBINSON, *History of Western Europe*, I, pp. 270–277.
ROBINSON, *Introduction to the History of Western Europe*, pp. 337–339, 347–352.
SCHEVILL, *Political History of Modern Europe*, pp. 5–15.
STILLÉ, *Studies in Medieval History*, ch. 15.

18. The Evolution of Spain and Portugal

THATCHER AND MCNEAL, *Europe in the Middle Age,* pp. 445-455.
THORNDIKE, *History of Medieval Europe,* pp. 341-371.

Supplementary References:
ABBOTT, *Expansion of Europe,* I, pp. 64-108; CHEYNEY, *European Background of American History,* chs. 1-4; CHEYNEY, *Industrial and Social History of England,* ch. 4; CUNNINGHAM, *Western Civilization in Its Economic Aspects,* II, pp. 62-82, 107-137, 154-182; CUTTS, *Scenes and Characters of the Middle Ages,* pp. 461-517; DAVIS, *Medieval Europe,* pp. 235-251; EMERTON, *Beginnings of Modern Europe,* pp. 187-199; *History of All Nations,* X, ch. 4; LODGE, *The Close of the Middle Ages,* ch. 18; MERRIMAN, *The Rise of the Spanish Empire,* I, pp. 171-237; MUNRO, *The Middle Ages,* ch. 29; OGG, *Economic Development of Modern Europe,* ch. 4; WEBSTER, *General History of Commerce,* chs. 9-13; ZIMMERN, *The Hansa Towns,* periods I-II.

Source Readings:
OGG, *Source Book of Mediæval History,* pp. 325-339; ROBINSON, *Readings in European History,* I, pp. 415-428; THATCHER AND MCNEAL, *Source Book for Mediæval History,* pp. 579-582.

B. MONARCHISTIC TENDENCIES IN EUROPEAN POLITICS.

18. The Evolution of Spain and Portugal.
    a. Complex Origin of Hispanic Peoples.
        i. Successive waves of invasion.
        ii. The development of a hybrid people.
    b. Religion as a line of Cleavage.
        i. Expansion of the Christian Marches.
            (a) Steps in the Christian recovery of the peninsula.
            (b) Final success of Ferdinand and Isabella.
        ii. Emergence of a new nation-state.
        iii. Effects of the expulsion of Moors and Jews.
    c. Types of Spanish Institutions.
        i. Rise of the *cortes.*
        ii. Government centralization under Ferdinand.
        iii. Fitness of Spain for colonization.
    d. The Separate Origin of Portugal.
    e. Portuguese Institutions: national feeling.

Turner, *Europe, 1450-1789,* pp. 56-57, 313-345.

19. Asiatic Influences on Eastern Europe

Parallel References:
ABBOTT, *Expansion of Europe*, I, pp. 113, 123–128.
BÉMONT AND MONOD, *Medieval Europe*, pp. 44, 104, 114, 155–156, 351, 476–479.
ROBINSON, *History of Western Europe*, I, pp. 93, 336–340, 352–355.
ROBINSON, *Introduction to the History of Western Europe*, pp. 83, 356–359, *passim*.
THORNDIKE, *History of Medieval Europe*, pp. 178–190, 270–273, 302–305, 630–633.

Supplementary References:
ABBOTT, *Expansion of Europe*, I, ch. 6; CHAPMAN, *History of Spain*, pp. 1–52, 67–83, 202–209, *passim*; *History of All Nations*, X, ch. 15; HUME, *Spain: Its Greatness and Decay*, chs. 1–3; JOHNSON, *Europe in the Sixteenth Century*, pp. 96–101; MERRIMAN, *The Rise of the Spanish Empire*, I, pp. 94–139, 383–425; MUNRO, *The Middle Ages*, pp. 104, 214, 387–391; PRESCOTT, *Ferdinand and Isabella*; STEPHENS, *The Story of Portugal*; WATTS, *The Christian Recovery of Spain*.

Illustrative Reading:
IRVING, *The Alhambra*, and *The Conquest of Granada*.

19. Asiatic Influences on Eastern Europe.
a. The Long Struggle between East and West.
   i. Westward movement of oriental peoples in ancient times: the Huns.
   ii. European inroads of the Magyars.
   iii. Irruptions of the Mongols.
      (a) Conquest and occupation of the Russian plain.
      (b) Destruction of the Seljuk Turks.
      (c) Origin of the Ottoman power.
b. Later Conquests of the Turks.
   i. Turkish conversion to Mohammedanism.
   ii. Attacks on the Byzantine Empire.
      (a) Partial conquest of the Balkan peninsula.
      (b) Fall of the Eastern Roman Empire: the Crusades.
   iii. The conquest of North Africa: Barbary States.
   iv. Control of the Eastern Mediterranean: Venice.
   v. Western limit of Turkish conquests: 1683.

20. Issues of the Hundred Years' War

c. Significance of the Ottoman Empire.
  i. Turkish hostility to cultural influences.
  ii. Islam under Turkish control.
  iii. Causes of Turkish decadence: European political problems.

Turner, *Europe, 1450-1789*, pp. 63--.

Parallel References:
ABBOTT, *Expansion of Europe*, I, pp. 10-11, 115-118, 204-205; II, pp. 67-71, 99-100.
HAYES, *Political and Social History of Modern Europe*, I, pp. 22-23, 80-81, 106, 383-384.
MUNRO, *The Middle Ages*, pp. 37-8, 45-6, 151, 397-400, ch. 22, *passim*.
ROBINSON, *History of Western Europe*, I, pp. 39, 41, 90-94, 122, 181, 214-215.
ROBINSON, *Introduction to the History of Western Europe*, pp. 25, 27, 149 *f.*, 509-511, 517-518.
TANNER, *The Renaissance and the Reformation*, ch. 7.
THORNDIKE, *History of Medieval Europe*, pp. 55-59, 548-551, 554-559.

Supplementary References:
BEAZLEY, FORBES, BIRKETT, *Russia from the Varangians to the Bolsheviks*, ch. 2; *Cambridge Mediæval History*, IV, chs. 20, 21; *Cambridge Modern History*, I, chs. 3, 8; CURTIN, *The Mongols in Russia, passim;* DAVIS, *Short History of the Near East*, chs. 3, 17-19, 22-24; *History of All Nations*, IX, ch. 20; OMAN, *The Story of the Byzantine Empire*, chs. 24-26; SCHEVILL, *The History of the Balkan Peninsula*, chs. 11-12.

20. Issues of the Hundred Years' War.

a. Causes of the Struggle.
  i. Territorial claims of English and French monarchs.
  ii. Conflicting interests in Flanders.
  iii. External causes of hatred: Scotland.
b. Character of the War.
  i. New and revolutionary methods of warfare.
  ii. Periods of the War.
    (a) Infrequent campaigns: results.
    (b) Destruction of French chivalry.
    (c) Recovery of France: Joan of Arc.
c. Social and Political Intermissions.
  i. The Black Death: labor troubles.
  ii. The Wars of the Roses.

21. Central Europe on the Eve of the Reformation

d. Results of the Century of Conflict.
  i. Decline of feudalism in France.
  ii. Loss of English possessions abroad: isolation.
  iii. Development of national sentiment.

Turner, *Europe, 1450-1789*, pp. 53-56, 362-376.

Parallel References:
ADAMS, *Civilization During the Middle Ages*, pp. 331-334
EMERTON, *Beginnings of Modern Europe*, ch. 6.
ROBINSON, *History of Western Europe*, I, pp. 170-178.
ROBINSON, *Introduction to the History of Western Europe*, pp. 277-302.
SEIGNOBOS, *History of Mediæval and Modern Civilization*, pp. 179-191.
STILLÉ, *Studies in Medieval History*, pp. 153-157, 233, 236.
THATCHER AND MCNEAL, *Europe in the Middle Age*, chs. 19-20.
THORNDIKE, *History of Medieval Europe*, ch. 27.

Supplementary References:
ADAMS, *Growth of the French Nation*, pp. 108-143; CHEYNEY, *Industrial and Social History of England*, ch. 5; CHEYNEY, *Short History of England*, chs. 10-11; CROSS, *History of England and Greater Britain*, chs. 12-16, *passim*; FUNCK-BRENTANO, *The Middle Ages*, ch. 19; HASSAL, *France, Medieval and Modern*, pp. 47-88; *History of All Nations*, X, chs. 3, 9; LARSON, *History of England and the British Commonwealth*, ch. 6, *passim*; LODGE, *The Close of the Middle Ages*, chs. 15-16; MASSON, *Mediæval France*, pp. 171-209.

Source Readings:
CHEYNEY, *Readings in English History*, pp. 233-267, 283-295; OGG, *Source Book of Mediæval History*, pp. 418-444; ROBINSON, *Readings in European History*, I, pp. 466-487.

21. Central Europe on the Eve of the Reformation.

a. Germany in the Sixteenth Century.
  i. Position of the Emperor: feudal prerogatives.
  ii. Government of the Empire.
    (a) Inclusiveness of the Empire.
    (b) Powers and functions of the Diet: the electors.
    (c) Inequalities in administration: the free cities.
    (d) Effects of the Great Interregnum.
  iii. Wretchedness of the German peasantry.
b. Rise of the Hapsburg Family.
  i. Origin of the Hapsburgs: territorial expansion.
  ii. The heritage of Charles V.

22. Religious Antecedents of the Reformation

c. The International Situation.
  i. The continuing feud of Empire and Papacy.
  ii. Rivalry with France: causes.
  iii. Italy as a European battleground.
  iv. Bearing of these troubles on the Reformation.

Turner, *Europe, 1450-1789*, pp. 242-262, 273-312, 373-378.

Parallel References:
ADAMS, *Civilization During the Middle Ages*, pp. 356-360, 406-416.
HAYES, *Political and Social History of Modern Europe*, I, pp. 74-91.
ROBINSON, *History of Western Europe*, I, pp. 341-364.
ROBINSON, *Introduction to the History of Western Europe*, pp. 354-375.
SCHEVILL, *Political History of Modern Europe*, pp. 25-70.
SEIGNOBOS, *History of Mediæval and Modern Civilization*, pp. 253-267.
SWINTON, *Outlines of History*, sec. V, pp. 317-325.
THORNDIKE, *History of Medieval Europe*, pp. 614-622, 633-639.

Supplementary References:
ABBOTT, *Expansion of Europe*, I, ch. 5; BRYCE, *Holy Roman Empire*, chs. 19-20; *Cambridge Modern History*, I, ch. 19; II, chs. 2-3; HENDERSON, *Short History of Germany*, I, pp. 264-272; *History of All Nations*, IX, ch. 16; X, chs. 2, 8; XI, ch. 1; HULME, *Renaissance and Reformation*, ch. 10; JOHNSON, *Europe in the 16th Century*, ch. 1, pp. 106-128; LINDSAY, *History of the Reformation*, I, pp. 51-94, 172-188; LODGE, *Close of the Middle Ages*, pp. 394-418, 468-493; TANNER, *The Renaissance and the Reformation*, chs. 4, 8-9.

Source Readings:
OGG, *Source Book of Mediæval History*, pp. 474-477; ROBINSON, *Readings in European History*, II, pp. 1-52; UNIVERSITY OF PENNSYLVANIA, *Translations and Reprints*, II, no. 6.

IV. THE REFORMATION AND POLITICAL READJUSTMENT

A. BEGINNINGS OF THE PROTESTANT UPHEAVAL.

22. Religious Antecedents of the Reformation.

a. The "Christian Renaissance."
  i. Re-translation and spread of the Scriptures.
  ii. Application of scholarship to religious writings.
  iii. Relation to the Reformation movement.

23. The Lutheran Revolt

  b. Types of Abuses in the Universal Church.
  i. Discrediting of the Papal Office.
   (a) Disputes at Rome: the Great Schism.
   (b) Babylonian Captivity of the Church.
   (c) Varying attitudes toward Papal Infallibility.
  ii. Moral and administrative evils.
   (a) Widespread corruption among the clergy.
   (b) Enervating effect of the wealth of the Church.
   (c) Doctrinal abuses: exploitation of indulgences.
  c. Forerunners of the Protestant Revolt.
  i. Work of the Humanists: Erasmus.
  ii. Premature revolts from the Church.
   (a) Wiclif and the Lollards.
   (b) The Hussite heresy.

Turner, *Europe, 1450-1789*, pp. 149-166.

Parallel References:
ABBOTT, *The Expansion of Europe*, I, pp. 186-192.
HAYES, *Political and Social History of Modern Europe*, I, pp. 112-124.
ROBINSON, *History of Western Europe*, I, pp. 365-384.
ROBINSON, *Introduction to the History of Western Europe*, pp. 375-386.
SEIGNOBOS, *History of Mediæval and Modern Civilization*, pp. 204-209, 383-4.
SCHEVILL, *Political History of Modern Europe*, pp. 44-55.
THORNDIKE, *History of Medieval Europe*, ch. 30, *passim*, pp. 633-639.

Supplementary References:
Cambridge Modern History, I, chs. 7, 17; II. ch. 1; FISHER, *The Reformation*, pp. 13-84; HENDERSON, *Short History of Germany*, I, pp. 203-227; *History of All Nations*, X, chs. 7, 8; HULME, *Renaissance and Reformation*, ch. 1; JOHNSON, *Europe in the 16th Century*, pp. 10-11, 25-33, 148-153; LINDSAY, *History of the Reformation*, I, ch. 5; SMITH, *The Age of the Reformation*, ch. 1; TANNER, *The Renaissance and the Reformation*, chs. 8-9; WALKER, *The Protestant Reformation*, pp. 45-55, 71-76.

Source Readings:
ROBINSON, *Readings in European History*, I, ch. 23.

23. The Lutheran Revolt.

  a. The Preparation for the German Reformation.
  i. Early career of Martin Luther.

24. The Epidemic Spread of Protestantism
      ii. Rise of the doctrinal issue.
          (a) Luther's pilgrimage to Rome.
          (b) The sale of indulgences: Tetzel.
     iii. Effect of the "ninety-five theses."
     iv. Rapid rise of controversy: Eck.
  b. From Controversy to Conflict.
      i. The breach: Luther's excommunication.
      ii. Champions of the new cause.
          (a) Luther's prestige as a university teacher.
          (b) "Address to the German Nobility."
     iii. The Diet of Worms: edict of outlawry.
     iv. Preoccupation of the Emperor.
     v. The Diet of Speyer: origin of Protestantism.
     vi. Lutheranism as a political issue.

Turner, *Europe, 1450-1789*, pp. 166-172.

Parallel References:
Abbott, *Expansion of Europe*, I, pp. 190-196.
Adams, *Civilization During the Middle Ages*, pp. 416-432.
Hayes, *Political and Social History of Modern Europe*, I, pp. 112-133.
Robinson, *History of Western Europe*, I, pp. 365-409.
Robinson, *Introduction to the History of Western Europe*, pp. 387-416.
Seignobos, *History of Mediæval and Modern Civilization*, pp. 284-292.
Schevill, *Political History of Modern Europe*, pp. 59-72.

Supplementary References:
Cambridge Modern History, II, chs. 4-8; Fisher, *The Reformation*, pp. 85-116; Henderson, *Short History of Germany*, I, pp. 251-263, 272-314; *History of All Nations*, XI, chs. 2-3; Hulme, *Renaissance and Reformation*, chs. 11-12, 14; Johnson, *Europe in the Sixteenth Century*, ch. 3; Lindsay, *History of the Reformation*, I, pp. 189-314; Smith, *The Age of the Reformation*, pp. 62-115; Tanner, *The Renaissance and the Reformation*, ch. 10; Walker, *The Protestant Reformation*, pp. 77-129.

Source Readings:
Robinson, *Readings in European History*, II, ch. 25; University of Pennsylvania, *Translations and Reprints*, II, no. 6.

B. PROGRESS OF THE REFORMATION MOVEMENT.
24. The Epidemic Spread of Protestantism.
  a. Progress of the Movement in Germany.
      i. Conversion of southern Germany: reasons.
      ii. Revolt of the peasants: consequent reaction.

24. The Epidemic Spread of Protestantism

    iii. The Protestant definition of faith.
        (a) Melancthon and the Augsburg Confession.
        (b) Attitude of the Humanists: Erasmus.
  b. Organization of Religious Parties.
    i. The Schmalkaldic and Catholic Leagues.
    ii. Character of the Schmalkaldic War.
    iii. The Religious Peace of Augsburg.
  c. New Centers of Protestantism.
    i. Political basis of the Swiss Reformation.
    ii. Teachings of Zwingli: the Swiss War.
    iii. Calvin and the origin of Presbyterianism.
        (a) Geneva as a center of instruction: the *Institutes*.
        (b) Rapid spread of Calvinistic doctrines.
    iv. The Reformation in Scotland: John Knox.

Turner, *Europe, 1450-1789*, pp. 173-182.

Parallel References:
ABBOTT, *Expansion of Europe*, I, pp. 199–206, 207–209, 211–215.
HAYES, *Political and Social History of Modern Europe*, I, pp. 133–148.
ROBINSON, *History of Western Europe*, I, pp. 409–444.
ROBINSON, *Introduction to the History of Western Europe*, pp. 416–426.
SCHEVILL, *Political History of Modern Europe*, pp. 73–97.
SEIGNOBOS, *History of Mediæval and Modern Civilization*, pp. 292–304.

Supplementary References:
Cambridge Modern History, II, chs. 10–11; FISHER, *The Reformation*, pp. 156–169; HENDERSON, *Short History of Germany*, I, pp. 289–307; *History of All Nations*, XI, chs. 4–6, 8–10; HULME, *Renaissance and Reformation*, chs. 13, 15–16; JOHNSON, *Europe in the Sixteenth Century*, chs. 4–5; LARSON, *History of England and the British Commonwealth*, pp. 307–315; LINDSAY, *History of the Reformation*, I, pp. 95–113, 326–399; SMITH, *The Age of Reformation*, pp. 116–181; TANNER, *The Renaissance and the Reformation*, chs. 11–14; WALKER, *The Protestant Reformation*, pp. 129–216, 225–276.

Source Readings:
ROBINSON, *Readings in European History*, II, pp. 94–134; UNIVERSITY OF PENNSYLVANIA, *Translations and Reprints*, III, no. 3.

25. The English Reformation

25. The English Reformation.
   a. Background of the English Revolt.
      i. Royal power of the Tudors: Henry VII.
      ii. Henry VIII and the Church.
         (a) Henry as "Defender of the Faith."
         (b) Rise of marital difficulties.
         (c) Wolsey and the divorce question.
         (d) The Act of Supremacy: schism in the Church.
   b. The Transition to Protestantism.
      i. Dissolution of the monasteries: motives.
      ii. The Act of Uniformity: enforcement.
      iii. Changes under Edward VI.
         (a) The Six Articles.
         (b) Establishment of a Church of England.
   c. Temporary Reaction under Mary Tudor.
      i. The Spanish Alliance.
      ii. The Marian persecutions: relative failure.

Turner, *Europe, 1450-1789,* pp. 182-184, 217, 411-427.

Parallel References:
ABBOTT, *Expansion of Modern Europe,* I, ch. 8, *passim.*
CHEYNEY, *Short History of England,* ch. 12.
HAYES, *Political and Social History of Modern Europe,* I, pp. 148-156.
ROBINSON, *History of Western Europe,* I, pp. 444-458.
ROBINSON, *Introduction to the History of Western Europe,* pp. 426-436.
SCHEVILL, *Political History of Modern Europe,* pp. 40-43, 119-141.

Supplementary References:
Cambridge Modern History, I, ch. 14; II, chs. 13-16; CHEYNEY, *European Background of American History,* ch. 11; CROSS, *History of England and Greater Britain,* chs. 18-23; FISHER, *History of the Reformation,* pp. 316-384; GREEN, *Short History of the English People,* pp. 303-369; *History of All Nations,* XI, ch. 13; LARSON, *History of England and the British Commonwealth,* pp. 262-306; SMITH, *The Age of the Reformation,* pp. 277-324; TANNER, *The Renaissance and the Reformation,* ch. 13; TOUT, *History of Great Britain,* pp. 308-367; WALKER, *The Protestant Reformation,* pp. 308-312.

Source Readings:
CHEYNEY, *Readings in English History,* pp. 267-271, ch. 12; ROBINSON, *Readings in European History,* II, pp. 135-155; UNIVERSITY OF PENNSYLVANIA, *Translations and Reprints,* I, no. 1.

26. The Maintenance of English Independence.

a. Reëstablishment of the English Church.
  i. The accession of Elizabeth: handicaps.
  ii. Necessity for a Protestant régime.
  iii. Efforts to secure religious uniformity.
b. Political Difficulties of the Reign.
  i. Catholic plots: fate of Mary Stuart.
  ii. Rise of Protestant non-conformists.
  iii. Liberalism and patriotism of Elizabeth's rule.
c. Foreign Policy: the Test of the Reformation.
  i. English intervention in the Netherlands.
  ii. Spanish aggression: defeat of the Great Armada.
  iii. Beginnings of English naval supremacy.
d. Culture of the Elizabethan era.
  i. Patronage of the royal court.
  ii. Vigor and worth of Elizabethan literature.

Turner, *Europe, 1450-1789*, pp. 221-222, 427-433.

Parallel References:
  ABBOTT, *Expansion of Europe*, I, chs. 14-15.
  CHEYNEY, *Short History of England*, ch. 13.
  HAYES, *Political and Social History of Modern Europe*, I, pp. 98-101, 155-156, *passim.*
  ROBINSON, *History of Western Europe*, I, pp. 479-488.
  ROBINSON, *Introduction to the History of Western Europe*, pp. 458-464.
  SCHEVILL, *Political History of Modern Europe*, pp. 114, 141-156.
  SEIGNOBOS, *History of Mediæval and Modern Civilization*, pp. 330-336.

Supplementary References:
  Cambridge Modern History, III, chs. 8-11; CROSS, *History of England and Greater Britain*, chs. 24-26; GREEN, *Short History of the English People*, pp. 369-420: *History of All Nations*, XI, ch. 15; LARSON, *History of England and the British Commonwealth*, pp. 306-343; LINDSAY, *History of the Reformation*, II, 274-314, 385-420; SMITH, *The Age of the Reformation*, pp. 329-349; WALKER, *The Protestant Reformation*, pp. 312-334, 432-439.

Source Readings:
  CHEYNEY, *Readings in English History*, ch. 13; ROBINSON, *Readings in European History*, II, pp. 186-199.

27. Philip II and the Revolt of the Netherlands

C. RELIGIOUS AND POLITICAL READJUSTMENT.
27. **Philip II and the Revolt of the Netherlands.**
   a. The Catholic Counter Reformation.
      i. Threat to the Universal Church of the Protestant revolt.
      ii. Necessity for counter action: means.
         (a) Serious divisions among the Protestants.
         (b) The Jesuits and the Inquisition.
         (c) The Council of Trent: purging of the Church.
   b. Background of the Revolt of the Netherlands.
      i. Political History of the Netherlands.
         (a) Evolution during the feudal age.
         (b) Transfer from Austria to Spain: Charles V.
      ii. Causes of the Religious Outbreak.
         (a) Influence of Protestant ideas.
         (b) Intolerance of Philip II: the Inquisition.
         (c) Ruin of industry: economic motives.
   c. Phases of the Revolt.
      i. Spanish invasion: the "Council of Blood."
      ii. Beginnings of Dutch naval power: "Sea Beggars."
      iii. The Union of Utrecht: partial success.
      iv. Final Dutch independence in 1648.

Turner, *Europe, 1450-1789*, pp. 180-181, 220-222, 237, 337-340, 343-344, 488.

Parallel References:
ABBOTT, *Expansion of Europe*, I, chs. 11-12.
HAYES, *Political and Social History of Modern Europe*, I, pp. 91-97, 156-169.
ROBINSON, *History of Western Europe*, I, pp. 459-473.
ROBINSON, *Introduction to the History of Western Europe*, pp. 437-451.
SCHEVILL, *Political History of Modern Europe*, pp. 97-114, 157-177.
SEIGNOBOS, *History of Mediæval and Modern Civilization*, pp. 324-330, ch. 21.

Supplementary References:
Cambridge Modern History, II, ch. 18; III, chs. 6-7, 15-16; FISHER, *History of the Reformation*, ch. 11; HENDERSON, *Short History of Germany*, I, pp. 395-421; *History of All Nations*, XI, chs. 12, 14; HULME, *Renaissance and Reformation*, chs. 20-22,

28. Dynastic and Religious Wars in France

25; JOHNSON, *Europe in the Sixteenth Century*, chs. 6–8; LINDSAY, *History of the Reformation*, II, pp. 525–611; LODGE, *History of Modern Europe*, ch. 8; SMITH, *The Age of the Reformation*, ch. 8; TANNER, *The Renaissance and the Reformation*, chs. 15–16; WALKER, *The Protestant Reformation*, ch. 9.

Source Readings:
ROBINSON, *Readings in European History*, II, pp. 156–179.

28. Dynastic and Religious Wars in France.
a. Beginnings of the Reformation in France.
   i. Spread of Calvinistic ideas.
   ii. Numbers and strength of the Huguenots.
   iii. The confused political situation.
      (a) Rival cliques in the royal family.
      (b) Rapid succession of the last Valois princes.
b. The Huguenot Wars.
   i. First attacks: reciprocal raids.
   ii. The massacre of St. Bartholomew's Day.
   iii. A period of irregular warfare: issues involved.
c. The Edict of Nantes.
   i. Accession of Henry IV: conditions.
   ii. Arranging of a religious truce: edict of toleration.
   iii. Significance of Bourbon rule: centralization.
d. The Last Phase: Richelieu.
   i. Final crushing of the Huguenots.
   ii. Consolidation of the French monarchy.

Turner, *Europe, 1450-1789*, pp. 184-185, 217-220, 222-226, 237-238, 376-387, 394-395.

Parallel References:
ABBOTT, *Expansion of Europe*, I, pp. 214, 282, 296–297, 428–429; II, pp. 97–98.
HAYES, *Political and Social History of Modern Europe*, I, pp. 101–106.
ROBINSON, *History of Western Europe*, I, pp. 473–479, 494 *ff*.
ROBINSON, *Introduction to the History of Western Europe*, pp. 451–458, 495.
SCHEVILL, *Political History of Modern Europe*, pp. 178–202.
SEIGNOBOS, *History of Mediæval and Modern Civilization*, pp. 336–344.

29. The Thirty Years' War in Germany

Supplementary References:
ADAMS, *Growth of the French Nation*, ch. 11; *Cambridge Modern History*, III, chs. 1–2, 20; IV, ch. 4; *History of All Nations*, XI, chs. 11, 15; XII, ch. 7; HULME, *Renaissance and Reformation*, chs. 16, 26; JOHNSON, *Europe in the Sixteenth Century*, ch. 9; LINDSAY, *History of the Reformation*, II, pp. 217–223, 274–314; LODGE, *History of Modern Europe*, pp. 101–125; SMITH, *The Age of the Reformation*, ch. 4; TANNER, *The Renaissance and the Reformation*, ch. 17; WALKER, *The Protestant Reformation*, pp. 312–334.

Source Readings:
ROBINSON, *Readings in European History*, II, pp. 179–186; UNIVERSITY OF PENNSYLVANIA, *Translations and Reprints*, III, no. 3.

29. The Thirty Years' War in Germany.
   a. Germany at the Opening of the War.
      i. Religious and political causes of conflict.
      ii. The organization of political parties.
         (a) Protestant and Catholic Leagues.
         (b) Ratios and centers of strength.
   b. Phases of the War.
      i. The Bohemian period: English neutrality.
      ii. The futility of Danish intervention.
      iii. Vicissitudes of the Swedish period.
      iv. Intervention of France: general exhaustion.
   c. The End of the Reformation.
      i. Total devastation of Germany: return to barbarism.
      ii. Economic ruin of all parties.
      iii. The Peace of Westphalia.
         (a) Religious terms: *cf.* the Religious Peace of Augsburg.
         (b) A general political settlement for Europe.

Turner, *Europe, 1450-1789*, pp. 228-237, 265-268, 573-575.

Parallel References:
ABBOTT, *Expansion of Europe*, I, ch. 19.
HAYES, *Political and Social History of Modern Europe*, I, pp. 218–232.
ROBINSON, *History of Western Europe*, I, pp. 489–497.
ROBINSON, *Introduction to the History of Western Europe*, pp. 465–474.

30. The Stuarts as "Divine Right" Rulers

SCHEVILL, *Political History of Modern Europe*, pp. 203-227.

Supplementary References:
BRYCE, *The Holy Roman Empire*, pp. 384-395; *Cambridge Modern History*, IV, chs. 1, 3, 5, 13, 14; GARDINER, *The Thirty Years' War*; HENDERSON, *A Short History of Germany*, I, chs. 17-18; *History of All Nations*, XII, chs. 1-2, 4-6, 8; XIII, ch. 2; LODGE, *History of Modern Europe*, ch. 10; WAKEMAN, *Europe, 1598-1715*, chs. 5-6; WALKER, *The Protestant Reformation*, pp. 439-460.

Source Readings:
ROBINSON, *Readings in European History*, II, pp. 200-218.

V. EVOLUTION OF A EUROPEAN STATES SYSTEM

A. ENGLISH EXPERIMENTS IN PERSONAL GOVERNMENT.

30. The Stuarts as "Divine Right" Rulers.
   a. Stuart Conception of the Kingship.
   b. James I as a Typical Stuart Sovereign.
   c. The Conflict between King and Parliament.
      i. Rise of the middle classes: Puritan ideas.
      ii. Persecution of non-conformists: emigration.
      iii. Religious aspects of foreign policy.
   d. The Difficulties of Charles I.
      i. Laud and the High Church movement.
      ii. Troubles with Scotland.
      iii. The Petition of Right: constitutional significance.
      iv. The question of taxes: personal government.
      v. Convening of the Long Parliament.
         (a) The "Bishops' Wars" with the Scots.
         (b) Failure of the Short Parliament.

Turner, *Europe, 1450-1789*, pp. 433-436.

Parallel References:
ABBOTT, *Expansion of Europe*, I, pp. 385-387, 396-401, 423, 429-430, *passim*.
HAYES, *Political and Social History of Modern Europe*, I, pp. 261-276.
HAZEN, *Modern Europe*, pp. 1-11.
ROBINSON, *History of Western Europe*, I, pp. 498-506.

31. Modified Republicanism: Commonwealth and Protectorate

    ROBINSON, *Introduction to the History of Western Europe*, pp. 475-485.
    SCHEVILL, *Political History of Modern Europe*, pp. 231-255.
    SEIGNOBOS, *History of Mediæval and Modern Civilization*, pp. 387-394.

    Supplementary References:
    Cambridge Modern History, III, ch. 22; IV, chs. 8-9; CHEYNEY, *Short History of England*, ch. 14; CROSS, *History of England and Greater Britain*, chs. 27-28; GREEN, *Short History of the English People*, pp. 474-535; *History of All Nations*, XIII, ch. 1; LARSON, *History of England and the British Commonwealth*, ch. 13.

    Source Readings:
    CHEYNEY, *Readings in English History*, ch. 14; ROBINSON, *Readings in European History*, II, pp. 218-239.

31. Modified Republicanism: Commonwealth and Protectorate.

  a. The Resort to War.
    i. Formation of hostile parties: Cavaliers and Roundheads.
    ii. Parliamentary measures: appearance of Cromwell.
    iii. Developments of the War: decisive battles.
    iv. Beginning of the interregnum.
      (a) Trial and execution of Charles I.
      (b) Dictatorship of the army.
  b. The Creation of a Commonwealth.
    i. The machinery of government: party factions.
    ii. War with the Irish and the Scotch.
    iii. Parliamentary troubles: the Rump Parliament.
  c. The Return to Personal Government.
    i. The Protectorate: "Instrument of Government."
    ii. End of Parliamentary government.
    iii. Increase of prestige abroad: the Dutch War.
    iv. Death of Cromwell: end of the experiment.

Turner, *Europe, 1450-1789*, pp. 436-440.

Parallel References:
    ABBOTT, *Expansion of Europe*, I, pp. 497-499, 502-505, 511-512.
    HAZEN, *Modern Europe*, pp. 11-24.
    HAYES, *Political and Social History of Modern Europe*, I, pp. 276-281.

32. The Restoration and the "Glorious Revolution"

ROBINSON, *History of Western Europe*, I, pp. 506–512.
ROBINSON, *Introduction to the History of Western Europe*, pp. 485–490.
SCHEVILL, *Political History of Modern Europe*, pp. 255–262.

Supplementary References:
Cambridge Modern History, IV, chs. 10–11, 15–16; V, ch. 11; CHEYNEY, *Short History of England*, ch. 15; CROSS, *History of England and Greater Britain*, chs. 29–31; GARDINER, *Oliver Cromwell*; GREEN, *Short History of the English People*, pp. 535–566; *History of All Nations*, XIII, ch. 1; LARSON, *History of England and the British Commonwealth*, ch. 14.

Source Readings:
CHEYNEY, *Readings in English History*, ch. 15; ROBINSON, *Readings in European History*, II, pp. 239–252.

32. The Restoration and the "Glorious Revolution."

a. The Stuart Restoration.
  i. The recall of Charles II: popular joy.
  ii. Dissolution of the Long Parliament: new legislation.
b. Renewed Difficulties with Parliament.
  i. Persecution of non-conformists.
  ii. New attempts at arbitrary government.
    (a) Financial issues: the Great Fire of 1666.
    (b) Foreign policy: the secret French alliance.
  iii. Charles' growing unpopularity: timely death.
c. The Reign of James II.
  i. Outcropping of old questions: political parties.
  ii. Factors suggesting a revolution.
d. The "Bloodless Revolution."
  i. The invitation to William and Mary.
  ii. The Declaration and the Bill of Rights.
  iii. First elements of cabinet government.

Turner, *Europe, 1450-1789*, pp. 440–446.

Parallel References:
ABBOTT, *Expansion of Europe*, II, ch. 25, *passim*.
HAYES, *Political and Social History of Modern Europe*, I, pp. 281–288.
HAZEN, *Modern Europe*, pp. 25–26.
ROBINSON, *History of Western Europe*, I, pp. 512–518.
ROBINSON, *Introduction to the History of Western Europe*, pp. 490–494.

33. Recovery of the French Monarchy

SCHEVILL, *Political History of Modern Europe*, pp. 261–273.

SEIGNOBOS, *History of Mediæval and Modern Civilization*, pp. 394–399.

Supplementary References:
Cambridge Modern History, V, chs. 5, 7–10; CHEYNEY, *Short History of England*, ch. 16; CROSS, *History of England and Greater Britain*, chs. 32–37; GREEN, *Short History of England*, ch. 9; *History of All Nations*, XIII, ch. 8; LARSON, *History of England and the British Commonwealth*, chs. 15–16; OGG, *Governments of Europe*, ch. 2.

Source Readings:
CHEYNEY, *Readings in English History*, ch. 16; ROBINSON, *Readings in European History*, II, pp. 252–263.

B. THE ACCOMPANIMENTS OF DESPOTISM IN FRANCE.

33. Recovery of the French Monarchy.
a. Basis of the Power of Louis the Magnificent.
  i. Outcome of the Huguenot wars.
  ii. Revocation of the Edict of Nantes.
  iii. Constructive work of Richelieu and Mazarin.
b. French Expansion in Europe.
  i. The doctrine of "Natural Boundaries."
  ii. Methods of territorial acquisition.
  iii. Encroachment in the Netherlands.
  iv. Nibbling on German territories.
c. The Struggle for the Balance of Power.
  i. The Spanish situation.
  ii. War of the Spanish Succession.
    (a) Powers involved in the contest.
    (b) Colonial phases of the war.
  iii. The Treaty of Utrecht.
    (a) Provisions concerning Franco-Spanish union.
    (b) Adjustments of territory.
  iv. Effects on French power and prestige.

Turner, *Europe, 1450-1789*, pp. 344-350, 380-388.

Parallel References:
ABBOTT, *Expanison of Europe*, I, pp. 428–429; II, pp. 51–52, 53–66.
HAYES, *Political and Social History of Modern Europe*, I, pp. 209–218.

34. The Age of Louis XIV

Hazen, *Modern Europe*, pp. 27-34, 42-48.
Robinson and Beard, *Development of Modern Europe*, I, ch. 2.
Robinson, *History of Western Europe*, I, pp. 519-524, 527-528.
Robinson and Beard, *Development of Modern Europe*, I, ch. 2.
Robinson, *Introduction to the History of Western Europe*, pp. 495-496, 501-507.
Schevill, *Political History of Modern Europe*, pp. 274-276, 278-287.
Seignobos, *History of Mediæval and Modern Civilization*, pp. 369-386.

Supplementary References:
Adams, *Growth of the French Nation*, ch. 12; *Cambridge Modern History*, IV, chs. 4, 21; V, chs. 2, 14; *History of All Nations*, XIII, chs. 4, 7, 10, 11; Johnson, *Age of the Enlightened Despot*, chs. 2-3; Lodge, *History of Modern Europe*, ch. 11; Perkins, *France under the Regency*, chs. 2, 6-9; Wakeman, *Europe, 1598-1715*, chs. 2, 6-7, 10-15.

Source Readings:
Robinson, *Readings in European History*, II, pp. 268-272, 293-297; Robinson and Beard, *Readings in Modern European History*, I, pp. 15-27.

34. The Age of Louis XIV.
   a. Domestic Policies of the Régime.
      i. Pinnacle of the "Divine Right" tenet.
      ii. Centralization of the Administration.
         (a) Enervation of the nobility.
         (b) Royal appointment and control of officials.
      iii. The reforms and doctrines of Colbert.
         (a) Financial administrative reforms.
         (b) Development of the mercantile doctrine.
   b. Social Conditions of the Period.
      i. Continued religious persecution.
      ii. The royal court at Versailles: envy of kings.
      iii. Brilliance of art and literature.
      iv. Cultural influences of the reign.
   c. The Close of the Age.
      i. Similar reign of Louis XV: corruption.
      ii. Ruinous effects of war on France.
      iii. Preparation for the Revolution.

Turner, *Europe, 1450-1789*, pp. 388-410.

35. The Emergence of Russia

Parallel References:
ABBOTT, *Expansion of Europe*, II, pp. 73-81.
HAYES, *Political and Social History of Modern Europe*, I, pp. 235-256.
HAZEN, *Modern Europe*, pp. 34-47.
ROBINSON AND BEARD, *Development of Modern Europe*, I, ch. 1.
ROBINSON, *History of Western Europe*, I, pp. 524-531.
ROBINSON, *Introduction to the History of Western Europe*, pp. 496-501, 507-8.
SCHEVILL, *Political History of Modern Europe*, pp. 276-278, 287-288.
SEIGNOBOS, *History of Mediæval and Modern Civilization*, pp. 406-418, 345-368.

Supplementary References:
ADAMS, *Growth of the French Nation*, ch. 13; *Cambridge Modern History*, V, chs. 1, 3, 4; *History of All Nations*, XIII, chs. 6-7; XIV, ch. 1; JOHNSON, *Age of the Enlightened Despot*, ch. 1; LODGE, *History of Modern Europe*, ch. 13; LODGE, *Richelieu*; PERKINS, *France under the Regency*, chs. 4-5; WAKEMAN, *Ascendancy of France*, ch. 9.

Source Readings:
ROBINSON, *Readings in European History*, II, pp. 273-293; ROBINSON AND BEARD, *Readings in Modern European History*, I, pp. 1-14.

C. CHANGES IN THE EUROPEAN POLITICAL FAMILY.

35. The Emergence of Russia.

a. Foundations of the Russian Kingdom.
  i. The physical and racial basis.
  ii. The early connection with Asia.
     (a) Adoption of the Greek Orthodox creed.
     (b) Effects of long Mongol domination.
  iii. Slow development of a Slavic Empire: the Romanoffs.
b. Services of Peter the Great.
  i. Expansion of the Russian domain.
     (a) Conquests from Turkey.
     (b) Acquisition of Baltic lands: Sweden.
  ii. The program of modernization.
     (a) Travels of the Czar: adoption of European methods.
     (b) Centralization of Church and State: the Streltsi.

36. Origin and Rise of the Prussian Kingdom
  c. Policies of Catherine II.
    i. The medieval character of domestic policy.
    ii. Consistent aggression in foreign affairs.
      (a) Wars with Turkey.
      (b) Intervention in Poland.

Turner, *Europe, 1450-1789*, pp. 95-98, 647-665.

Parallel References:
ABBOTT, *Expansion of Europe*, I, pp. 114-115, 286, 300-301, 309-310, 401-402; II, pp. 4-5, 159 *ff*.
HAYES, *Political and Social History of Modern Europe*, I, pp. 20-23, 366-374.
HAZEN, *Modern Europe*, pp. 69-77.
ROBINSON AND BEARD, *Development of Modern Europe*, I, pp. 50-55, 74-79, 187.
ROBINSON, *Introduction to the History of Western Europe*, pp. 509-515.
SCHEVILL, *Political History of Modern Europe*, pp. 289-301.

Supplementary References:
BEAZLEY, FORBES, BIRKETT, *Russia from the Varangians to the Bolsheviks*, bks. I-II; BURY, *Catherine II*; *Cambridge Modern History*, I, chs. 3, 10; V, chs. 16-17; VI, chs. 10, 19; HASSAL, *The Balance of Power*, chs. 5, 11; *History of All Nations*, XIV, ch. 3; JOHNSON, *Age of the Enlightened Despot*, chs. 4-5; LODGE, *History of Modern Europe*, pp. 186, 187, 267-287; MOTLEY, *Peter the Great*; MUNRO, *The Middle Ages*, pp. 391-401; WAKEMAN, *Ascendancy of France*, pp. 289-310.

Source Readings:
ROBINSON, *Readings in European History*, II, pp. 301-315; ROBINSON AND BEARD, *Readings in Modern European History*, I, pp. 57-63.

36. Origin and Rise of the Prussian Kingdom.
  a. Rise of the House of Hohenzollern.
    i. Early connection with Brandenburg.
    ii. Inheritance of East Prussia: royal title.
    iii. Expansion of Brandenburg-Prussia: the "Great Elector."
    iv. Development of Prussian prestige.
      (a) Succession of able rulers: Frederick William I.
      (b) Economic basis of future greatness: expansion.
      (c) Emphasis on military life and sentiment.

37. Austria and the Extinction of Poland

b. Developments of the Reign of Frederick II.
   i. The Silesian Question.
       (a) The Austrian Pragmatic Sanction: its violation.
       (b) The War of the Austrian Succession: extent.
       (c) The far-reaching treaty of Aix-la-Chapelle.
   ii. Features of the Seven Years' War.
       (a) The Diplomatic Revolution.
       (b) World-wide extent of the struggle.
       (c) The Treaty of Hubertsburg and the Peace of Paris.
       (d) Important results of the war.

Turner, *Europe, 1450-1789*, pp. 268, 270, 350-353, 587-602.

Parallel References:
HAYES, *Political and Social History of Modern Europe*, I, pp. 347-362.
HAZEN, *Modern Europe*, pp. 59-69.
ROBINSON AND BEARD, *Development of Modern Europe*, I, pp. 55-71.
ROBINSON, *Introduction to the History of Western Europe*, pp. 515-522.
SCHEVILL, *Political History of Modern Europe*, pp. 302-322.

Supplementary References:
ABBOTT, *Expansion of Europe*, I, p. 300; II, pp. 15-18, chs. 30, 32; *Cambridge Modern History*, V, chs. 20-21; VI, chs. 8-9; CARLYLE, *Frederick the Great*; HENDERSON, *Short History of Germany*, II, chs. 1-5; *History of All Nations*, XIV, chs. 7-8; XV, chs. 1-3, 5, 8; JOHNSON, *Age of the Enlightened Despot*, chs. 6-8; LODGE, *History of Modern Europe*, chs. 17-19; SCHEVILL, *The Making of Modern Germany*, chs. 1-2.

Source Readings:
ROBINSON, *Readings in European History*, II, pp. 315-328; ROBINSON AND BEARD, *Readings in Modern European History*, I, pp. 61-82.

37. Austria and the Extinction of Poland.

a. The Leadership of Austria in Germany.
   i. Connection with the Holy Roman Empire.
   ii. Relations with Bohemia and Hungary.
   iii. The difficult position of Maria Theresa.

37. Austria and the Extinction of Poland

b. The Political Situation in Poland.
  i. Origin and rise of the state.
  ii. Inherent causes of weakness.
    (a) Lack of natural frontiers.
    (b) Numbers and power of the nobility.
  iii. Foreign interference in Polish government.
c. The Partitions of Poland.
  i. Source of the partition plot: Austrian reluctance.
  ii. Parties in the division of spoil: motives.
  iii. Attempted Polish reform: Kosciusko.
  iv. The disappearance of Poland.
    (a) Unsatisfactory results: artificiality of the awards.
    (b) Persistence of the Polish Question.

Turner: *Europe, 1450-1789,* pp. 45-46, 590-592, 629-647.

Parallel References:
ABBOTT, *Expansion of Europe,* II, pp. 67-68, 103, 159-161, 286-287.
HAYES, *Political and Social History of Modern Europe,* I, pp. 381-388, *passim.*
HAZEN, *Modern Europe,* pp. 59-60, 80-83.
ROBINSON, *Introduction to the History of Western Europe,* pp. 578 *f.*, 521, 583-4.
ROBINSON AND BEARD, *Development of Modern Europe,* I, pp. 71-79.
SCHEVILL, *Political History of Modern Europe,* pp. 294-296, 298, 300.

Supplementary References:
BARN, *Slavonic Europe,* chs. 5-19; BEAZLEY, FORBES, BIRKETT, *Russia from the Varangians to the Bolsheviks,* bk. II, ch. 3; *Cambridge Modern History,* VI, chs. 7, 20; GIBBONS, *The New Map of Europe,* ch. 6; HASSAL, *The Balance of Power,* chs. 4-5, 10; HENDERSON, *Short History of Germany,* II, ch. 4; *History of All Nations,* XIV, ch. 5; XV, ch. 6; JOHNSON, *Age of the Enlightened Despot,* chs. 9-10; LODGE, *Modern Europe,* ch. 18; PHILLIPS, *Poland,* chs. 1-6.

Source Readings:
ROBINSON, *Readings in European History,* II, pp. 325 *ff.*;
ROBINSON AND BEARD, *Readings in Modern European History,* I, pp. 82-89, 239-242.

38. The Commercial Revolution

VI. COMMERCIALISM AND THE NEW PHILOSOPHY

A. STRUGGLES FOR COLONIAL SUPREMACY.

38. The Commercial Revolution.
   a. Factors Contributing to a New Commercial Era.
      i. Character and extent of the medieval trade.
      ii. Rise of a new interest in trade.
         (a) Growth of European populations: causes.
         (b) National support of commercial enterprise.
   b. Characteristics of the Commercial Revolution.
      i. Search for water routes to the East Indies.
         (a) Motives for exploring activities: pepper.
         (b) Opening of the route around Africa.
      ii. Discoveries in the western hemisphere.
      iii. Relation of commercial expansion to the modern era.
   c. Theories of Trade Control.
      i. Rise of the doctrine of mercantilism: Colbert.
         (a) Belief that "trade follows the flag."
         (b) Attempts at monopoly in trade and colonization.
      ii. Types of colonies: corporation efforts.

Turner, *Europe, 1450-1789*, pp. 58-61, 531-534, 710-717.

Parallel References:
CHEYNEY, *Industrial and Social History of England*, pp. 63-81, 138-147.
HAYES, *Political and Social History of Modern Europe*, I, pp. 43-54, 196-201.
ROBINSON, *Introduction to the History of Western Europe*, pp. 199, 243-249, 302.
ROBINSON AND BEARD, *Development of Modern Europe*, I, pp. 11, 80; II, p. 49.
SCHEVILL, *Political History of Modern Europe*, pp. 10-13, 278.

Supplementary References:
ABBOTT, *Expansion of Europe*, I, pp. 253-274; BOLTON AND MARSHALL, *Colonization of North America*, ch. 1; CHEYNEY, *European Background of American History*, chs. 1-3; MUIR, *Expansion of Europe*, ch. 1; OGG, *Economic Development of Modern Europe*, ch. 4; WEBSTER, *General History of Commerce*,

39. Beginnings of Colonial Expansion

ch. 14; WOODWARD, *Expansion of the British Empire*, chs. 1–2; ZIMMERN, *The Hansa Towns*, Period III.

Source Readings:
ROBINSON AND BEARD, *Readings in Modern European History*, I, pp. 13–14, 90–93.

39. Beginnings of Colonial Expansion.
a. Establishments of the Portuguese.
   i. Insular and African way stations: value.
   ii. Temporary hegemony in the Far East.
b. Rise of Spanish Dominions.
   i. Early date of Spanish beginnings.
   ii. Rise of the Spanish American Empire.
      (a) Conquest of the mainland: Mexico and Peru.
      (b) Effect of American gold on Europe.
      (c) Types of Spanish colonial control: evils.
   iii. Permanent effects of Spanish enterprise.
c. Later Appearance of Northern European Nations.
   i. Aggressiveness of the Dutch.
      (a) Acquisition of East Indian territories.
      (b) Successful coping with European rivals.
   ii. First Efforts of the English.
      (a) Difficult beginnings in America.
      (b) Success of the East India Company.
   iii. Location and extent of early French activities.

Turner, *Europe, 1450-1789*, pp. 534-555.

Parallel References:
CHEYNEY, *Industrial and Social History of England*, pp. 163–167, *passim*.
HAYES, *Political and Social History of Modern Europe*, I, pp. 55–62.
ROBINSON AND BEARD, *Development of Modern Europe*, I, pp. 80–87.
SCHEVILL, *Political History of Modern Europe*, pp. 13–15, *passim*.
SEIGNOBOS, *History of Contemporary Civilization*, pp. 29–42.

Supplementary References:
ABBOTT, *Expansion of Europe*, I, chs. 3, 6, 9; BOLTON AND MARSHALL, *Colonization of North America*, chs. 2–3; CHEYNEY, *European Background of American History*, chs. 4–5; KELLER, *Colonization*, chs. 1–6, 10–11; MUIR, *Expansion of Europe*,

40. The Colonial Duel of England and France

ch. 2; WEBSTER, *General History of Commerce*, chs. 15–17; WOODWARD, *Expansion of the British Empire*, chs. 3–4.

Source Readings:
ROBINSON, *Readings in European History*, II, pp. 331–335; ROBINSON AND BEARD, *Readings in Modern European History*, I, pp. 93–101.

40. The Colonial Duel of England and France.
a. Rival Interests in America.
  i. Motives for settlement: character and influence.
  ii. Contrasts in colonial establishments.
  iii. Reasons for the conflict in America.
b. Preliminary and Indecisive Colonial Wars.
  i. Their relation to European struggles.
  ii. The American Indian as a factor.
  iii. Counter maneuvers in India.
  iv. Preparations for a final contest.
c. The Decisive Conflict.
  i. The French and Indian War in America.
    (a) Plans of campaigns: determining factors.
    (b) Success of American colonial and British forces.
  ii. The War in India.
    (a) Importance of sea power.
    (b) Strategic battles: Clive and Plassey.
  iii. The wide bearing of the outcome.

Turner, *Europe, 1450–1789,* pp. 350–351, 402–405, 524–527, 551–558.

Parallel References:
CHEYNEY, *Short History of England*, ch. 17, pp. 436–451.
HAYES, *Political and Social History of Modern Europe*, I, pp. 299–306, 312–320.
HAZEN, *Modern Europe*, pp. 52–53, *passim.*
ROBINSON, *Introduction to the History of Western Europe*, pp. 527–532.
ROBINSON AND BEARD, *Development of Modern Europe*, I, pp. 87–111.
SCHEVILL, *Political History of Modern Europe*, pp. 336–338.
SEIGNOBOS, *History of Contemporary Civilization*, pp. 42–47.

41. Revolution within the British Empire

Supplementary References:
ABBOTT, *Expansion of Europe*, II, chs. 28-32; BOLTON AND MARSHALL, *Colonization of North America*, chs. 4-5, 14-20; *Cambridge Modern History*, VI, chs. 13, 15; VII, chs. 1-4; CROSS, *History of England and Greater Britain*, ch. 41; LARSON, *History of England and the British Commonwealth*, ch. 17; MUIR, *Expansion of Europe*, ch. 3; THWAITES, *France in America*, chs. 6-17; WEBSTER, *General History of Commerce*, chs. 19-20; WOODWARD, *Expansion of the British Empire*, ch. 5.

Source Readings:
CHEYNEY, *Readings in English History*, pp. 590-603; ROBINSON, *Readings in European History*, II, pp. 335-344; ROBINSON AND BEARD, *Readings in Modern European History*, I, pp. 101-130.

41. **Revolution within the British Empire.**
    a. Background of the Revolution.
        i. Nature of the American colonies: laxity of control.
        ii. Economic interests of the colonies.
            (a) Growth of colonial trade.
            (b) Tardy enforcement of the mercantile policy.
        iii. Rapid development of the colonies: conscious strength.
        iv. Blunders in statesmanship: the issue.
    b. Revolt of the American Colonies.
        i. Organization of the colonies: leadership.
        ii. Eventual failure of English military campaigns.
        iii. Timely foreign aid: end of the struggle.
    c. Important Results of the Revolution.
        i. Changes in British government and colonial policy.
        ii. Influence on European politics.
        iii. Beginning of a new type of state.

Turner, *Europe, 1450-1789*, pp. 558-564, *passim.*

Parallel References:
CHEYNEY, *Short History of England*, ch. 18.
HAYES, *Political and Social History of Modern Europe*, I, pp. 322-340.
HAZEN, *Modern Europe*, pp. 53-56.
ROBINSON, *Introduction to the History of Western Europe*, pp. 532-535.
ROBINSON AND BEARD, *Development of Modern Europe*, I, pp. 111-121.

42. English Constitutional Development

Schevill, *Political History of Modern Europe*, p. 339 (inadequate).
Seignobos, *History of Contemporary Civilization*, pp. 47-54.

Supplementary References:
Abbott, *Expansion of Europe*, ch. 35; Bolton and Marshall, *Colonization of North America*, chs. 23-27; *Cambridge Modern History*, VII, chs. 5-7; Cross, *History of England and Greater Britain*, chs. 42-43; Hassal, *The Balance of Power, 1715-1789*, ch. 12; *History of All Nations*, XIV, ch. 2; XV, ch. 9; Larson, *History of England and the British Commonwealth*, ch. 19; Muir, *Expansion of Europe*, ch. 4; Woodward, *Expansion of the British Empire*, ch. 6.

Source Readings:
Cheyney, *Readings in English History*, pp. 616-646; Robinson, *Readings in European History*, II, pp. 353-356; Robinson and Beard, *Readings in Modern European History*, I, pp. 130-137, 242-244.

B. THE PATH OF MODERN PROGRESS.

42. English Constitutional Development.
a. The Peculiar Development of England.
  i. Political effects of isolation.
  ii. Slow evolution of liberal institutions.
  iii. England as a "political laboratory" for the world.
b. Accomplishments of the Eighteenth Century.
  i. Constitutional bases of English Government.
  ii. Beginnings of party (cabinet) government.
    (a) Incompetence of the early Hanoverians.
    (b) Growth of the cabinet: party unity.
c. Need of Further Political Change.
  i. Faulty representation in Parliament.
  ii. Agitation for reform: William Pitt (the Younger).
  iii. Influence of the American Revolution.
  iv. Effects of the French Revolution.
    (a) Paralyzing of the reform program.
    (b) Postponement of action until 1832.
  v. Social and industrial conditions.

Turner, *Europe, 1450-1789*, pp. 508-527.

Parallel References:
Hayes, *Political and Social History of Modern Europe*, I, pp. 288-293, 430-440.

43. Opening of the Age of Reason

Hazen, *Modern Europe*, pp. 49-52.
Robinson, *Introduction to the History of Western Europe*, pp. 523-527.
Robinson and Beard, *Development of Modern Europe*, I, pp. 195-201.
Schevill, *Political History of Modern Europe*, pp. 323-340.
Seignobos, *History of Mediæval and Modern Civilization*, pp. 399-405.

Supplementary References:
Abbott, *Expansion of Europe*, II, ch. 34; Cheyney, *Short History of England*, ch. 17; Cross, *History of England and Greater Britain*, chs. 44-45; Green, *Short History of the English People*, pp. 701-745; Larson, *History of England and the British Commonwealth*, ch. 20; Munro, *Governments of Europe*, chs. 1-2; Ogg, *Governments of Europe*, ch. 3; Slater, *The Making of Modern England*, (Introduction), chs. 1-2; Trevelyan, *British History in the Nineteenth Century*, chs. 1-2, 4.

Source Readings:
Cheyney, *Readings in English History*, ch. 17; Robinson and Beard, *Readings in Modern European History*, I, pp. 220-224.

43. Opening of the Age of Reason.

a. The Decline of Religious Uniformity.
  i. The heritage of the Reformation: new sects.
  ii. Relation of philosophy and religion: free thinking.
  iii. Steps toward freedom of conscience: England and America.
b. Eighteenth Century Political Ideals.
  i. Political theories: vogue of Machiavellian principles.
  ii. The cult of "enlightened" or "benevolent" despotism.
    (a) Identification of dynasties with national growth.
    (b) Decline of popular assemblies on the continent.
    (c) Typical enlightened despots and their work.
  iii. International relations: balance of power.
c. Mainstays of the Old Régime.
  i. Recovered influence of the Catholic Church.
  ii. Popular ignorance: absence of systematic education.

44. The Eighteenth Century Scientific Movement

   iii. Economic slavery of the masses.
   iv. Lack of leadership: influence of French philosophers.

Turner, *Europe, 1450-1789*, pp. 668-725.

Parallel References:
Hayes, *Political ana Social History of Modern Europe*, I, pp. 395-414.
Hazen, *Modern Europe*, pp. 77-83.
Robinson and Beard, *Development of Modern Europe*, I, pp. 167-201.
Schapiro, *Modern and Contemporary European History*, pp. 1-4.
Schevill, *Political History of Modern Europe*, pp. 21-24, pt. II, *passim*.
Seignobos, *History of Contemporary Civilization*, pp. 75-91.

Supplementary References:
Abbott, *Expansion of Europe*, II, ch. 31; Bourne, *The Revolutionary Period in Europe*, ch. 4; *Cambridge Modern History*, V, ch. 23; VI, ch. 23; VIII, ch. 1; Hassal, *The Balance of Power, 1715-1789*, ch. 13; *History of All Nations*, XIV, ch. 9; XV, ch. 7; Johnson, *Age of the Enlightened Despot*, ch. 10, pp. 254-259; Lodge, *History of Modern Europe*, ch. 20; Lowell, *Eve of the French Revolution*, ch. 23; Rose, *The Revolutionary and Napoleonic Era*, pp. 1-21; Stephens, *Revolutionary Europe, 1789-1815*, ch. 1.

Source Readings:
Robinson, *Readings in European History*, II, pp. 380-386; Robinson and Beard, *Readings in Modern European History*, pp. 200-225; University of Pennsylvania, *Translations and Reprints*, VI.

44. The Eighteenth Century Scientific Movement.
  a. Cumulative Effects of Scientific Knowledge.
    i. Origins of the sciences.
      (a) Evolution of mathematics and astronomy.
      (b) Development of the physical sciences.
      (c) Founders of the natural sciences.
    ii. From science to philosophy.
      (a) The scientific basis of philosophic speculation.
      (b) Attempts to socialize science.
  b. Forerunners of a New Social and Political Order.
    i. The Teachings of Voltaire: cynicism.

45. The *Ancien Régime*
    ii. The social gospel of Rousseau.
    iii. Contributions of Beccaria, Diderot, Montesquieu.
  c. The Rise of a New Economy.
    i. Theories of the mercantilists.
    ii. The *laisser faire* advocates: Malthus, Turgot, Adam Smith.
  d. Symptoms of the New Thought.
    i. Expression in art and literature.
    ii. Bearing on the philosophy of the French Revolution.

Turner, *Europe, 1450-1789*, pp. 725-738.

Parallel References:
HAYES, *Political and Social History of Modern Europe*, I, pp. 414-426.
HAZEN, *Modern Europe*, pp. 105-112.
ROBINSON, *Introduction to the History of Western Europe*, pp. 548-552.
ROBINSON AND BEARD, *Development of Modern Europe*, I, pp. 157-166.
SCHAPIRO, *Modern and Contemporary European History*, pp. 7-8.
SCHEVILL, *Political History of Modern Europe*, pp. 350-353, *passim*.
SEIGNOBOS, *History of Contemporary Civilization*, pp. 55-75.

Supplementary References:
ABBOTT, *Expansion of Europe*, II, ch. 33; ADAMS, *Growth of the French Nation*, ch. 14; BOURNE, *The Revolutionary Period in Europe*, ch. 3; *Cambridge Modern History*, VIII, ch. 1; HASSAL, *The Balance of Power, 1715-1789*, pp. 412-419; *History of All Nations*, XV, ch. 4; JOHNSON, *Age of the Enlightened Despot, passim*; LOWELL, *Eve of the French Revolution*, chs. 5, 10, 16-19; ROSE, *The Revolutionary and Napoleonic Era*, pp. 21-29; STEPHENS, *Revolutionary Europe, 1789-1815*, Introduction.

Source Readings:
ROBINSON AND BEARD, *Readings in Modern European History*, I, pp. 179-199; University of Pennsylvania, *Translations and Reprints*, VI, No. 1, pp. 2-27.

45. The *Ancien Régime*.
  a. The Backwardness of Europe.
    i. Survivals of feudalism.
      (a) Prevalence of serfdom on the continent.

45. The Ancien Régime

      (b) Feudal basis of agriculture and industry: methods.
  ii. Standing abuses of the old order.
      (a) Adjuncts of autocracy: vested interests and exemptions.
      (b) Slow rise of the *bourgeoisie:* burdens.
b. The *Ancien Régime* in France.
  i. Prerogatives of king and nobles.
  ii. Extravagance of the royal court: Versailles.
  iii. Wealth and indolence of the clergy.
  iv. Poverty and wretchedness of the lower classes.
c. Evils of Administration in France.
  i. The variety of burdensome taxes.
  ii. Irregularity of legal codes.
  iii. Restiveness of the *Tiers État.*

Turner, *Europe Since 1789,* **pp. 1-42.**

Parallel References:
Hayes, *Political and Social History of Modern Europe,* I, pp. 449-458.
Hazen, *Modern Europe,* pp. 84-105.
Robinson, *Introduction to the History of Western Europe,* pp. 537-548.
Robinson and Beard, *Development of Modern Europe,* I, ch. 11.
Schevill, *Political History of Modern Europe,* pp. 344-352.
Seignobos, *History of Contemporary Civilization,* pp. 92-106.

Supplementary References:
Adams, *Growth of the French Nation,* chs. 14-15; Bourne, *Revolutionary Period in Europe,* chs. 1-2; *Cambridge Modern History,* VIII, chs. 1, 4; Hassal, *The Balance of Power, 1715-1789,* pp. 401-412, 419-424; *History of All Nations,* XIV, ch. 3; Johnson, *Age of the Enlightened Despot,* ch. 9; Lodge, *History of Modern Europe,* pp. 484-488; Lowell, *Eve of the French Revolution,* chs. 1-4, 6-9, 14-15; Mathews, *The French Revolution,* pp. 1-51.

Source Readings:
Robinson, *Readings in European History,* II, pp. 360-380; Robinson and Beard, *Readings in Modern European History,* I, pp. 138-171; University of Pennsylvania, *Translations and Reprints,* I, no. 5; Young, *Travels in France.*

46. Beginnings of the French Revolution

VII. THE FRENCH REVOLUTIONARY CYCLE
A. THE PERIOD OF THE REVOLUTION.
46. Beginnings of the French Revolution.
   a. The Heritage of Louis XVI.
      i. Extravagances of previous reigns.
      ii. "*Après nous, le déluge.*"
   b. The Accession of Louis XVI.
      i. Character of the royal family: "*Madame Déficit.*"
      ii. Incapacity of Louis.
   c. Efforts to Avoid National Bankruptcy.
      i. Weakening of national credit: size of the debt.
      ii. Economic measures of Turgot and Necker.
      iii. The disastrous remedy of Calonne.
   d. Summoning of the Estates General.
      i. Failure of the Assembly of Notables.
      ii. Composition of the Estates General.
      iii. Hostility of King and nobles.
      iv. Radical tendencies: vote *par tête*.
      v. Revolutionary forebodings: the National Assembly.

Turner, *Europe Since 1789*, pp. 42-48.

Parallel References:
HAYES, *Political and Social History of Modern Europe*, I, pp. 458–468.
HAZEN, *Modern Europe*, pp. 113–126.
ROBINSON, *Introduction to the History of Western Europe*, pp. 553–563.
ROBINSON AND BEARD, *Development of Modern Europe*, I, pp. 224–233.
SCHEVILL, *Political History of Modern Europe*, pp. 352–354.
SEIGNOBOS, *History of Contemporary Civilization*, pp. 106–120.

Supplementary References:
ADAMS, *Growth of the French Nation*, pp. 272–277; BOURNE, *The Revolutionary Period in Europe*, ch. 7; *Cambridge Modern History*, VIII, chs. 5–6; *History of All Nations*, XV, ch. 9; XVI, ch. 2; LODGE, *History of Modern Europe*, pp. 488–495; MATHEWS, *The French Revolution*, pp. 102–124; ROSE, *The*

47. The Trial of Limited Monarchy

Revolutionary and Napoleonic Era, chs. 2–3; STEPHENS, *Revolutionary Europe*, *1789–1815*, ch. 2.

Source Readings:
ANDERSON, *Constitutions and Documents*, pp. 1–11; ROBINSON, *Readings in European History*, II, pp. 386–404; ROBINSON AND BEARD, *Readings in Modern European History*, I, pp. 235–239, 244–247; UNIVERSITY OF PENNSYLVANIA, *Translations and Reprints*, VI, no. 1, pp. 32–35; IV, no. 5.

47. The Trial of Limited Monarchy.
   a. Progress of the Revolutionary Movement.
      i. Capture of the Bastille, July 14: significance.
      ii. The "Abolition of Privileges," August 4–5.
      iii. Indications of a counter revolution.
      iv. The "Triumphal Entry" of October 5–6.
      v. Dominating influence of the Paris populace.
   b. Formation of a Constitution.
      i. Origin of constitutional ideas and theories.
      ii. The Declaration of the Rights of Man.
      iii. Completion of the Constitution.
         (a) Character and importance of the document.
         (b) End of the Assembly: Self-denying Ordinance.
   c. The Legislative Assembly: Its Problems.
      i. Defects in the Constitution.
      ii. Rise of foreign complications.
      iii. Domestic difficulties: growing radicalism.
      iv. Break-down of constitutional monarchy.

Turner, *Europe Since 1789*, pp. 48–56.

Parallel References:
HAYES, *Political and Social History of Modern Europe*, I, pp. 468–500.
HAZEN, *Modern Europe*, pp. 126–174.
ROBINSON, *Introduction to the History of Western Europe*, pp. 563–573.
ROBINSON AND BEARD, *Development of Modern Europe*, I, pp. 233–263.
SCHAPIRO, *Modern and Contemporary European History*, pp. 8–11.
SCHEVILL, *Political History of Modern Europe*, pp. 354–369.
SEIGNOBOS, *History of Contemporary Civilization*, pp. 121–131.

48. Experiments with Democracy: the Convention

Supplementary References:
ADAMS, *Growth of the French Nation*, pp. 277–289; BOURNE, *Revolutionary Period in Europe*, chs. 8–10; *Cambridge Modern History*, VIII, chs. 7–8, 10–11; *History of All Nations*, XVI, ch. 3; LODGE, *History of Modern Europe*, pp. 511–537; LOWELL, *Eve of the French Revolution*, chs. 3–5; MATHEWS, *The French Revolution*, pp. 125–220; OGG, *Economic Development of Modern Europe*, pp. 92–98, 187–198; ROSE, *The Revolutionary and Napoleonic Era*, ch. 4; STEPHENS, *Revolutionary Europe, 1789–1815*, ch. 3.

Source Readings:
ANDERSON, *Constitutions and Documents*, pp. 11–128; ROBINSON, *Readings in European History*, II, pp. 404–446; ROBINSON AND BEARD, *Readings in Modern European History*, I, pp. 248–294; UNIVERSITY OF PENNSYLVANIA, *Translations and Reprints*, I, no. 5.

48. Experiments with Democracy: the Convention.
a. End of the Monarchy.
   i. Growing suspicion of the royal family.
      (a) Attempts to escape: correspondence.
      (b) Incompetence of Louis XVI.
   ii. Popular insurrections: rise of parties.
   iii. Trial and execution of King and Queen.
   iv. Proclamation of a Republic, September 22, 1792.
b. The Provisional Government.
   i. The Constitution of 1793.
   ii. Facing of foreign perils.
      (a) *Émigrés* and the invasion of France.
      (b) Emergency measures: *levée en masse*.
      (c) Domestic safety through Terror.
      (d) Services and abuses of the Terror régime.
c. Return to Stable Government.
   i. Constitution of the Year III: provisions.
   ii. Significance of the Convention.

Turner, *Europe Since 1789*, pp. 56-66.

Parallel References:
FUETER, *World History, 1815–1920*, pp. 11–21.
HAYES, *Political and Social History of Modern Europe*, I, pp. 500–512.
HAZEN, *Modern Europe*, pp. 175–207.
ROBINSON, *Introduction to the History of Western Europe*, pp. 574–591.

49. Formation of the Empire

ROBINSON AND BEARD, *Development of Modern Europe*, I, pp. 263–282.
SCHEVILL, *Political History of Modern Europe*, pp. 369–383.
SEIGNOBOS, *History of Contemporary Civilization*, pp. 131–144.

Supplementary References:
ADAMS, *Growth of the French Nation*, pp. 289–307; BOURNE, *Revolutionary Period in Europe*, chs. 11–13; *Cambridge Modern History*, VIII, chs. 9, 12–15; FYFFE, *History of Modern Europe*, chs. 1–2; *History of All Nations*, XVI, chs. 4–5; LODGE, *History of Modern Europe*, pp. 538–553; MATHEWS, *The French Revolution*, pp. 220–285; ROSE, *The Revolutionary and Napoleonic Era*, ch. 5; STEPHENS, *Revolutionary Europe, 1789–1815*, chs. 4–5.

Source Readings:
ANDERSON, *Constitutions and Documents*, pp. 128–254; ROBINSON, *Readings in European History*, II, pp. 446–460; ROBINSON AND BEARD, *Readings in Modern European History*, I, pp. 295–308.

B. THE NAPOLEONIC PERIOD.

49. Formation of the Empire.

a. The Rise of Napoleon Bonaparte.
  i. The rising star: the 13th *Vendémiaire*.
  ii. The Directory: problems and personnel.
  iii. Fortunes of Napoleon's Italian campaign.
  iv. Results of the expedition to Egypt and Syria.
  v. The *coup d'état:* overthrow of the Directory.
b. Program of the Consulate.
  i. Constitution of the Year VIII.
  ii. War with the Second Coalition.
c. Inauguration of the Empire.
  i. The reconstruction of France.
    (a) Alliance with the Papacy.
    (b) Constructive works: the *Code Napoléon*.
  ii. Establishment of the Empire.
    (a) Crushing of all opposition.
    (b) Constitution of the new order.
  iii. Napoleon as Emperor.
    (a) Personal traits: relation to the Revolution.
    (b) Establishment of an imperial court.

Turner, *Europe Since 1789*, pp. 67-78.

50. Attempted Mastery of Europe

Parallel References:
HAYES, *Political and Social History of Modern Europe*, I, pp. 512–533.
HAZEN, *Modern Europe*, pp. 208–250.
ROBINSON, *Introduction to the History of Western Europe*, pp. 592–608.
ROBINSON AND BEARD, *Development of Modern Europe*, I, pp. 284–313.
SCHEVILL, *Political History of Modern Europe*, pp. 383–394.
SEIGNOBOS, *History of Contemporary Civilization*, pp. 144–169.

Supplementary References:
BOURNE, *Revolutionary Period in Europe*, chs. 14–20; *Cambridge Modern History*, VIII, chs. 16, 18–22, 25; IX, chs. 1–3; FYFFE, *History of Modern Europe*, chs. 3–5; *History of All Nations*, XVI, chs. 8–9; XVII, ch. 1; LODGE, *History of Modern Europe*, pp. 553–585; ROSE, *The Life of Napoleon I*, vol. I; ROSE, *The Revolutionary and Napoleonic Era*, chs. 6–7; STEPHENS, *Revolutionary Europe, 1789–1815*, chs. 6–7.

Source Readings:
ANDERSON, *Constitutions and Documents*, pp. 255–368; ROBINSON, *Readings in European History*, II, pp. 460–489; ROBINSON AND BEARD, *Readings in Modern European History*, I, pp. 309–332; UNIVERSITY OF PENNSYLVANIA, *Translations and Reprints*, II, no. 2.

50. **Attempted Mastery of Europe.**
   a. Foreign Affairs of the New Empire.
      i. Renewal of war with England.
      ii. The Third Coalition against France.
      iii. The Austrian campaign: victories.
   b. The Transformation of Germany.
      i. Rewards of devotion: creation of new royalties.
      ii. Confederation of the Rhine: end of the Holy Roman Empire.
   c. The Extension of Military Despotism.
      i. The war with Prussia: dismemberment.
      ii. The campaign against Russia: Tilsit.
      iii. Renewal of the war with Austria: Wagram.
   d. Application of the Continental System.
      i. Need of crushing England.
      ii. Economic policy: Berlin and Milan decrees.
      iii. Difficulties in enforcement: military pressure.

51. Decline and Fall of the Napoleonic Structure

e. Appearance of National Sentiment in Europe.
   i. Transition from political to national warfare.
   ii. Character of the Spanish uprising.
   iii. Ominous signs elsewhere: popular sentiment.

Turner, *Europe Since 1789*, pp. 78-86.

Parallel References:
Hayes, *Political and Social History of Modern Europe*, I, pp. 534-555.
Hazen, *Modern Europe*, pp. 251-285.
Robinson, *Introduction to the History of Western Europe*, pp. 608-620.
Robinson and Beard, *Development of Modern Europe*, I, pp. 313-332.
Schevill, *Political History of Modern Europe*, pp. 394-404.
Seignobos, *History of Contemporary Civilization*, pp. 170-185.

Supplementary References:
Bourne, *Revolutionary Period in Europe*, chs. 21-24; *Cambridge Modern History*, IX, chs. 5-6, 8-13; Fyffe, *History of Modern Europe*, chs. 6-9; *History of All Nations*, XVII, chs. 2-3; Lodge, *History of Modern Europe*, ch. 5, *passim*; Ogg, *Economic Development of Modern Europe*, pp. 99-112; Rose, *The Life of Napoleon I*, vol. II; Rose, *The Revolutionary and Napoleonic Era*, chs. 8-9; Stephens, *Revolutionary Europe, 1789-1815*, chs. 8-9.

Source Readings:
Anderson, *Constitutions and Documents*, pp. 368-424; Robinson, *Readings in European History*, II, pp. 490-514; Robinson and Beard, *Readings in Modern European History*, I, pp. 333-350; University of Pennsylvania, *Translations and Reprints*, II, no. 2.

51. Decline and Fall of the Napoleonic Structure.

a. Culmination of the Empire.
   i. The Hapsburg marriage.
   ii. Elements of weakness in the Empire.
b. Indications of Imperial Decadence.
   i. Rapid recovery of Spain and Prussia.
   ii. Economic distress: Church hostility.
   iii. The invasion of Russia: fatal result.
   iv. The "War of Liberation" of 1813.
      (a) Rising of the German states.
      (b) French defeats: decline of mass power.

52. The Revamping of Europe at Vienna

    c. Overthrow of the Napoleonic Order.
        i. Campaigns of 1814: "Battle of the Nations."
        ii. Capture of Paris: Napoleon's abdication.
    d. The Hundred Days.
        i. Circumstances favoring Napoleon's return.
        ii. The final campaign: Waterloo.
        iii. The end: St. Helena.

Turner, *Europe Since 1789*, pp. 86–92.

Parallel References:
HAYES, *Political and Social History of Modern Europe*, I, pp. 555–576.
HAZEN, *Modern Europe*, pp. 286–306.
ROBINSON, *Introduction to the History of Western Europe*, pp. 620–625.
ROBINSON AND BEARD, *Development of Modern Europe*, I, pp. 332–341.
SCHEVILL, *Political and Social History of Modern Europe*, pp. 402–413.
SEIGNOBOS, *History of Contemporary Civilization*, pp. 185–192.

Supplementary References:
BOURNE, *Revolutionary Period in Europe*, chs. 24–27; *Cambridge Modern History*, IX, chs. 15, 17, 20, 24; FOURNIER, *Life of Napoleon, passim*; FYFFE, *History of Modern Europe*, chs. 10–11; HENDERSON, *Short History of Germany*, II, pp. 270–296; *History of All Nations*, XVII, chs. 4–7; LODGE, *History of Modern Europe*, pp. 615–628; ROSE, *The Revolutionary and Napoleonic Era*, ch. 10; STEPHENS, *Revolutionary Europe, 1789–1815*, ch. 10.

Source Readings:
ANDERSON, *Constitutions and Documents*, pp. 424–480; ROBINSON, *Readings in European History*, II, pp. 514–529; ROBINSON AND BEARD, *Readings in Modern European History*, I, pp. 351–371; UNIVERSITY OF PENNSYLVANIA, *Translations and Reprints*, I, no. 5, pp. 2–9.

VIII. ALTERNATING REACTION AND REVOLUTION

A. THE PERIOD OF RETRENCHMENT.

    52. The Revamping of Europe at Vienna.
        a. Problems of the Congress.
            i. Personnel of the body: its leaders.
            ii. Aims and guiding principles.

52. The Revamping of Europe at Vienna

      iii. Conflicting interests: claims and counter claims.
      iv. Threats of war: effect of the Hundred Days.
  b. The Basis of a New Political Order.
      i. The isolation of France: buffer states.
      ii. Compensations for the Allies.
      iii. Application of the idea of "legitimacy."
      iv. The Holy Alliance.
         (a) The "moral association" of Alexander I.
         (b) Formation of the Quadruple Alliance: motives.
  c. Activities of the Congress.
      i. Informal negotiations of treaties and agreements.
      ii. Social activities in Vienna.

Turner, *Europe Since 1789*, pp. 93-102.

Parallel References:
HAYES, *Political and Social History of Modern Europe*, II, pp. 1-10.
HAZEN, *Europe Since 1815*, pp. 1-17.
HAZEN, *Modern Europe*, pp. 308-317.
ROBINSON, *Introduction to the History of Western Europe*, pp. 626-631.
ROBINSON AND BEARD, *Development of Modern Europe*, I, pp. 343-357.
SCHAPIRO, *Modern and Contemporary European History*, pp. 17-22.
SCHEVILL, *Political History of Modern Europe*, pp. 409, 414-418.
SEIGNOBOS, *History of Contemporary Civilization*, pp. 192-203.

Supplementary References:
Cambridge Modern History, IX, chs. 18-19, 21; FRESKA, *A Peace Congress of Intrigue*; FYFFE, *History of Modern Europe*, ch. 12; HAZEN, *Three Peace Congresses*; *History of All Nations*, XVIII, ch. 7; LODGE, *History of Modern Europe*, pp. 628-634; MALLESON, *The Life of Prince Metternich*; PHILLIPS, *Modern Europe, 1815-1899*, ch. 1; ROSE, *The Revolutionary and Napoleonic Era*, ch. 11; STEPHENS, *Revolutionary Europe, 1789-1815*, ch. 11.

Source Readings:
ANDERSON, *Constitutions and Documents*, pp. 480-485; ROBINSON, *Readings in European History*, II, pp. 533-536; ROBINSON AND BEARD, *Readings in Modern European History*, I, pp. 372-

53. The "Concert" of Europe

384; UNIVERSITY OF PENNSYLVANIA, *Translations and Reprints*, I, no. 3, pp. 8–14.

53. **The "Concert" of Europe.**
   a. Basis of the "Metternich System."
      i. Austria after the Congress of Vienna.
         (a) The prestige of Prince Metternich.
         (b) Austrian leadership in the Germanic Confederation.
      ii. Objects of the Quadruple Alliance.
         (a) Reaction as the basis for lasting peace.
         (b) International congresses: the doctrine of intervention.
   b. Applications of the System.
      i. Suppression of liberal ideas in Germany.
         (a) Return from constitutional government.
         (b) The Carlsbad Decrees: *Burschenschaften:* espionage.
      ii. Revolutionary outbursts in Spain and Portugal.
      iii. Italian movements in 1820: failure.
      iv. The failure of intervention.
         (a) England and the Monroe Doctrine.
         (b) French withdrawal from the Grand Alliance.

Turner, *Europe Since 1789,* **pp. 102-107.**

Parallel References:
FUETER, *World History, 1815–1920,* pp. 44–56.
HAYES, *Political and Social History of Modern Europe,* II, pp. 10–14, 20–28, 41–46.
HAZEN, *Europe Since 1815,* pp. 18–52.
HAZEN, *Modern Europe,* pp. 317–330.
ROBINSON, *Introduction to the History of Western Europe,* pp. 631–641.
ROBINSON AND BEARD, *Development of Modern Europe, I,* pp. 357–362.
SCHAPIRO, *Modern and Contemporary European History,* pp. 22–24.
SCHEVILL, *Political History of Modern Europe,* pp. 418–427.

Supplementary References:
Cambridge Modern History, X, chs. 1, 11; CRESSON, *The Holy Alliance: the European Background of the Monroe Doctrine;* FYFFE, *History of Modern Europe,* chs. 13–14; HART, *The Monroe*

54. The July Revolution in France

Doctrine, chs. 3-5; HAWKESWORTH, *The Last Century in Europe*, chs. 1-10; *History of All Nations*, XVIII, chs. 1-2; LODGE, *History of Modern Europe*, pp. 636-648; PHILLIPS, *Modern Europe, 1815-1899*, chs. 2-6; PHILLIPS, *The Confederation of Europe, passim.*

Source Readings:
ROBINSON, *Readings in European History*, II, pp. 543-557; ROBINSON AND BEARD, *Readings in Modern European History*, I, pp. 384-387; II, pp. 23-44; UNIVERSITY OF PENNSYLVANIA, *Translations and Reprints*, I, no. 3, pp. 14-24.

54. The July Revolution in France.
    a. Government of the Restored Bourbons.
        i. Establishment of the Revolution.
            (a) The Charter of 1814.
            (b) The moderate rule of Louis XVIII.
            (c) Activities of the "ultras."
        ii. Reactionary measures of Charles X.
            (a) Restoration of corrupt privileges.
            (b) Loss of popular support.
    b. The July Revolution.
        i. Attacks on the Charter: the July Ordinances.
        ii. The revolt of Paris.
        iii. Establishemnt of the Orleans Monarchy.
    c. Significance of the Revolution.
        i. Evidences of growing liberalism.
        ii. Effect on the tranquillity of Europe.

Turner, *Europe Since 1789*, pp. 107-108, 208-216.

Parallel References:
FUETER, *World History, 1815-1920*, pp. 57-68, 189-211.
HAYES, *Political and Social History of Modern Europe*, II, pp. 14-20, 50-53.
HAZEN, *Europe Since 1815*, pp. 71-97.
HAZEN, *Modern Europe*, pp. 366-375.
ROBINSON, *Introduction to the History of Western Europe*, pp. 642-646.
ROBINSON AND BEARD, *Development of Modern Europe*, II, pp. 1-10.
SCHAPIRO, *Modern and Contemporary European History*, pp. 89-97.
SCHEVILL, *Political History of Modern Europe*, pp. 428-432.

55. Revolutions beyond France in 1830

Supplementary References:
Cambridge Modern History, X, chs. 3, 15; DICKINSON, *Revolution and Reaction in Modern France;* FYFFE, *History of Modern Europe,* pp. 603–619; HALL, *The Bourbon Restoration;* HALL, *England and the Orleans Monarchy, passim; History of All Nations,* XVIII, chs. 6–8; LODGE, *History of Modern Europe,* pp. 657–662; PHILLIPS, *Modern Europe, 1815–1899,* ch. 8.

Source Readings:
ANDERSON, *Constitutions and Documents,* pp. 485–513; ROBINSON, *Readings in European History,* II, pp. 536–542; ROBINSON AND BEARD, *Readings in Modern European History,* II, pp. 2–14.

55. **Revolutions beyond France in 1830.**
   a. Effects of the July Revolution.
      i. Revolutionary symptoms broadcast.
      ii. Proposed intervention in France: failure.
   b. Weakness of the European Concert.
   c. Revolution in the Netherlands.
      i. Separation of Belgium from the Dutch Netherlands.
      ii. International guarantees of Belgian independence.
   d. The Struggle in Poland.
      i Polish dependence on French support.
      ii. Russian recovery: loss of the Constitution.
   e. Demonstrations in Germany and Italy.
      i. Effects of political disunion.
      ii. Success of the Metternich machine.
   f. The Reform Movement in England.
   g. Significance of Revolutionary Tendencies.

Turner, *Europe Since 1789,* pp. 97, 98, 108, 219, 156–158, 273–277.

Parallel References:
FUETER, *World History, 1815–1920,* pp. 69–81.
HAYES, *Political and Social History of Modern Europe,* II, pp. 46–50, 52–57.
HAZEN, *Europe Since 1815,* pp. 98–108.
HAZEN, *Modern Europe,* pp. 375–382.
ROBINSON, *Introduction to the History of Western Europe,* pp. 648–9, 686, 726 (inadequate).
ROBINSON AND BEARD, *Development of Modern Europe,* II, pp. 11–29.

56. Modern Industrial Beginnings

SCHAPIRO, *Modern and Contemporary European History*, pp. 59, 67–97, 201, 485–6.
SCHEVILL, *Political History of Modern Europe*, pp. 432–437.

Supplementary References:
Cambridge Modern History, X, chs. 3–4, 14; XI, chs. 3–4; DICKINSON, *Revolution and Reaction in Modern France;* FYFFE, *History of Modern Europe*, pp. 619–645; HALL, *England and the Orleans Monarchy; History of All Nations*, XVIII, chs. 9–10; LODGE, *History of Modern Europe*, pp. 663–672; PHILLIPS, *Modern Europe, 1815–1899*, ch. 9.

Source Readings:
MCBAIN AND ROGERS, *The New Constitutions of Europe*, pp. 499–520; ROBINSON, *Readings in European History*, II, pp. 557–558; ROBINSON AND BEARD, *Readings in Modern European History*, II, pp. 14–16.

B. THE INDUSTRIAL REVOLUTION.

56. Modern Industrial Beginnings.

a. The Slow Evolution of Industry.
   i. Dependence of civilization on industry.
   ii. Restrictive influences of industrial fixity.
b. Meaning of the Industrial Revolution.
   i. Rapidity of industrial development.
   ii. Changes in modern life: problems.
c. Revolutionary Mechanical Improvements.
   i. Beginnings of the movement in England: reasons.
   ii. The sequence of invention in cloth manufacture.
   iii. Accumulation of stresses in all industrial lines.
d. Application of Power to Manufacturing.
   i. Early use of water power.
   ii. Development and application of the steam engine.
   iii. The use of steam in transportation.
   iv. Scope of the new industrial movement.

Turner, *Europe Since 1789*, pp. 111–127.

Parallel References:
FUETER, *World History, 1815–1920*, pp. 7–10, 83–85, *passim*.
HAYES, *Political and Social History of Modern Europe*, II, pp. 65–75.
HAZEN, *Europe Since 1815*, pp. 53–70.

57. Features of the Factory System

Hazen, *Modern Europe*, pp. 331–336.
Robinson, *Introduction to the History of Western Europe*, pp. 677–680.
Robinson and Beard, *Development of Modern Europe*, II, pp. 30–44.
Schapiro, *Modern and Contemporary European History*, pp. 25–34.
Schevill, *Political History of Modern Europe*, pp. 530–536.

Supplementary References:
Bourne, *Revolutionary Period in Europe*, ch. 6; *Cambridge Modern History*, X, ch. 23; Cunningham, *The Growth of English Industry and Commerce*, III, pp. 609–628; Gibbins, *Industry in England*, chs. 20–22; Innes, *England's Industrial Development*; Ogg, *Economic Development of Modern Europe*, chs. 7, 11; Slater, *The Making of Modern England*, Introduction, chs. 2, 10; Toynbee, *Lectures on the Industrial Revolution of the Eighteenth Century*, pp. 1–57; Webster, *General History of Commerce*, chs. 21–27.

Source Readings:
Robinson, *Readings in European History*, II, pp. 599–613; Robinson and Beard, *Readings in Modern European History*, II, pp. 45–58.

57. **Features of the Factory System.**
   a. The Rise of Capitalism.
      i. The handicraft system of manufacture.
      ii. Early organization of industry: the domestic system.
      iii. Changes produced by the factory system.
   b. Character of Industrial Changes.
      i. The centralization of labor: the English enclosure movement.
      ii. Relation between production and consumption.
      iii. Expansion of trade and growth of markets.
         (a) Need of new sources of raw materials.
         (b) Beginnings of international market competition.
   c. New Social and Governmental Problems.
      i. The concentration of wealth: unearned incomes.
      ii. Rise of a new political economy: Adam Smith.
      iii. Appearance of the capitalistic state.
      iv. Organization of labor: trades unions.

58. The February Revolution of 1848
    v. Socialism: theories and experiments.
    vi. Effects on government: the spread of democracy.

Turner, *Europe Since 1789*, pp. 127-147.

Parallel References:
FUETER, *World History, 1815–1920*, pp. 85–89, 97*f.*, 193–198, 201–204, 381–402.
HAYES, *Political and Social History of Modern Europe*, II, pp. 75–97.
HAZEN, *Europe Since 1815*, pp. 257–281.
HAZEN, *Modern Europe*, pp. 337–338.
ROBINSON, *Introduction to the History of Western Europe*, pp. 680–684.
ROBINSON AND BEARD, *Development of Modern Europe*, II, pp. 44–52.
SCHAPIRO, *Modern and Contemporary European History*, pp. 34–44, 570–586.
SCHEVILL, *Political History of Modern Europe*, pp. 536–541.

Supplementary References:
Cambridge Modern History, X, chs. 23–24; CLARK, *The Effects of the Factory System*; GIBBINS, *Industry in England*, chs. 23–24; *History of All Nations*, XVIII, chs. 4–5; HOBSON, *The Evolution of Modern Capitalism*; INNES, *England's Industrial Development*; MACGREGOR, *The Evolution of Industry*; OGG, *Economic Development of Modern Europe*, chs. 6, 21; SLATER, *The Making of Modern England*, ch. 3; SPARGO, *Socialism*; TOYNBEE, *Lectures on the Industrial Revolution of the Eighteenth Century*, pp. 57–152.

Source Readings:
HAYES, *British Social Politics*, chs. 2–3; ROBINSON, *Readings in European History*, II, pp. 615–619; ROBINSON AND BEARD, *Readings in Modern European History*, II, pp. 58–72.

C. THE MID-CENTURY REVOLUTIONARY PERIOD.

58. The February Revolution of 1848.
    a. The Course of the July Monarchy.
        i. Strict attention to *bourgeois* interests.
        ii. Republican agitation: the "September Days" (1835).
        iii. Foreign relations of the monarchy.
            (a) The aggressive policy of Thiers: crisis of 1839–40.
            (b) The pacific program of Guizot.
        iv. Increasing unpopularity of the régime.

59. Revolutionary Movements in Central Europe

b. Downfall of the Orleans Monarchy.
  i. The "Reform Banquets" of 1848.
  ii. Overthrow of Louis Philippe.
c. Transition to a Republic.
  i. Rival parties: strength of the Socialists.
    (a) The program of Louis Blanc.
    (b) Merging of two provisional groups: Lamartine.
  ii. Work of the temporary régime.
  iii. Character of the new constitution.

Turner, *Europe Since 1789*, pp. 108-109, 216-225.

Parallel References:
FUETER, *World History, 1815–1920*, pp. 96, 174, 194–196, 248 f., *passim*.
HAYES, *Political and Social History of Modern Europe*, II, pp. 116–123.
HAZEN, *Europe Since 1815*, pp. 109–132.
HAZEN, *Modern Europe*, pp. 382–390.
ROBINSON, *Introduction to the History of Western Europe*, pp. 646–649.
ROBINSON AND BEARD, *Development of Modern Europe*, II, pp. 53–63.
SCHAPIRO, *Modern and Contemporary European History*, pp. 97–103.
SCHEVILL, *Political History of Modern Europe*, pp. 438–444.

Supplementary References:
Cambridge Modern History, XI, ch. 5; FISHER, *The Republican Tradition in Europe*, chs. 7–8; FYFFE, *History of Modern Europe*, pp. 699–706, 728–737; *History of All Nations*, XVIII, chs. 12–16; LODGE, *History of Modern Europe*, pp. 672–686; MARRIOTT, *The French Revolution of 1848 in Its Economic Aspects*, 2 vols.; OGG, *Economic Development of Modern Europe*, pp. 212–214, ch. 13; PHILLIPS, *Modern Europe, 1815–1899*, chs. 10–11.

Source Readings:
ANDERSON, *Constitutions and Documents*, pp. 513–537; ROBINSON, *Readings in European History*, II, pp. 559–562; ROBINSON AND BEARD, *Readings in Modern European History*, II, pp. 73–84.

59. Revolutionary Movements in Central Europe.

a. Popular Unrest in Central Europe.
  i. Cross currents: liberalism and nationalism.
  ii. The personification of difficulties in Metternich.
  iii. Remains of the Old Régime.

60. The Partial Triumph of Reaction

b. Overthrow of the Metternich System.
  i. The rising in Hungary: Deák and Kossuth.
  ii. The storm center in Vienna.
  iii. Revolutionary successes in Hungary and Bohemia: March Laws.
  iv. Revolt in the Austrian Provinces.
c. The March Days in Germany.
  i. The uprising in Berlin: royal promises.
  ii. Widespread granting of new constitutions.
  iii. Calling of the Frankfort Parliament.
d. Steps toward National Unity in Italy.
  i. Leadership of Sardinia–Piedmont: Charles Albert.
  ii. Partial coöperation of other Italian states.

Turner, *Europe Since 1789*, pp. 109, 234–251.

Parallel References:
FUETER, *World History, 1815–1920*, pp. 248, 279–284, 406–408.
HAYES, *Political and Social History of Modern Europe*, II, pp. 123–137.
HAZEN, *Europe Since 1815*, pp. 133–151.
HAZEN, *Modern Europe*, pp. 392–398.
ROBINSON, *Introduction to the History of Western Europe*. pp. 650–653.
ROBINSON AND BEARD, *Development of Modern Europe*, II, pp. 72–80.
SCHAPIRO, *Modern and Contemporary European History*, pp. 131–135.
SCHEVILL, *Political History of Modern Europe*, pp. 445–449.

Supplementary References:
Cambridge Modern History, XI, chs. 6–7; FYFFE, *History of Modern Europe*, pp. 707–728; HENDERSON, *Short History of Germany*, II, ch. 8; *History of All Nations*, XVIII, chs. 13–14; LODGE, *History of Modern Europe*, pp. 686–701; PHILLIPS, *Modern Europe, 1815–1899*, ch. 12.

Source Readings:
ROBINSON, *Readings in European History*, II, pp. 564–569; ROBINSON AND BEARD, *Readings in Modern European History*, II, pp. 95–101.

60. The Partial Triumph of Reaction.

a. Reactionary Gains in the Hapsburg Domain.
  i. The conquest of Bohemia.

60. The Partial Triumph of Reaction

    ii. Initial advances in Lombardy.
    iii. Rise of civil dissensions in Hungary: the minorities.
    iv. The conquest of Hungary: Russian aid.
    v. Divisions among the Italians.
    vi. Final Italian defeat: return of despotism.
  b. Restoration of the Old Order in Germany.
    i. Work of the Frankfort Parliament.
      (a) Problems to be solved: serious obstacles.
      (b) Tardy conclusion: failure of its purposes.
    ii. The "Humiliation of Olmütz."
    iii. Character of the reactionary government in Prussia.
  c. Net Results of Revolutionary Movements.
    i. Slight gains in constitutional governments.
    ii. Popular lessons drawn from revolts.

Turner, *Europe Since 1789*, pp. 251-258.

Parallel References:
FUETER, *World History, 1815-1920*, pp. 249-250, 285-288, *passim*.
HAYES, *Political and Social History of Modern Europe*, II, pp. 135-136, 137-144.
HAZEN, *Europe Since 1815*, pp. 152-165.
HAZEN, *Modern Europe*, pp. 398-406.
ROBINSON, *Introduction to the History of Western Europe*, pp. 653-658.
ROBINSON AND BEARD, *Development of Modern Europe*, II, pp. 80-89.
SCHAPIRO, *Modern and Contemporary European History*, pp. 135-144.
SCHEVILL, *Political History of Modern Europe*, pp. 449-457.

Supplementary References:
Cambridge Modern History, XI, ch. 15; FYFFE, *History of Modern Europe*, pp. 738-809; HENDERSON, *Short History of Germany*, II, pp. 370-410; *History of All Nations*, XVIII, ch. 15; LODGE, *History of Modern Europe*, pp. 701-732; MARRIOTT, *The Making of an Empire*; PHILLIPS, *Modern Europe, 1815-1899*, ch. 13.

Source Readings:
ROBINSON, *Readings in European History*, II, pp. 566-567, 569-572; ROBINSON AND BEARD, *Readings in Modern European History*, II, pp. 101-114.

61. Accretional Origin of the Italian Kingdom

IX. THE CENTRIPETAL INFLUENCES OF NATIONALISM
A. EMERGENCE OF THE ITALIAN NATION.
61. Accretional Origin of the Italian Kingdom.
   a. The Awakening of Italy (*Resorgimento*).
      i. National spirit aroused by Napoleonic control.
      ii. Common hostility to Austria.
      iii. Italian stirrings in 1820, 1830, 1848.
      iv. Counter interests of national and liberal elements.
   b. Plans for the Unification Process.
      i. Mazzini and the "Young Italy" Society.
      ii. Suggestions for Papal leadership: Pius IX.
   c. Developments toward Practical Organization.
      i. Rise of Sardinia-Piedmont.
      ii. The genius and policy of Cavour.
         (a) Economic reorganization and development.
         (b) Participation in the Crimean War.
      iii. The War of 1859 with Austria: results.
   d. Formation of the Kingdom of Italy.
      i. Annexation of Bourbon lands and Papal states: Garibaldi.
      ii. Proclamation of the new Kingdom.

Turner, *Europe Since 1789*, pp. 271-283.

Parallel References:
   Fueter, *World History, 1815-1920*, pp. 248-260.
   Hayes, *Political and Social History of Modern Europe*, II, pp. 124, 136, 139-150, 163-174.
   Hazen, *Europe Since 1815*, pp. 188-207.
   Hazen, *Modern Europe*, pp. 419-434.
   Holt and Chilton, *European History, 1862-1914*, pp. 43-49.
   Robinson and Beard, *Development of Modern Europe*, II, pp. 90-98.
   Schapiro, *Modern and Contemporary European History*, pp. 195-218.
   Schevill, *Political History of Modern Europe*, pp. 462-466.

Supplementary References:
   Cambridge Modern History, XI, ch. 14; Fyffe, *History of Modern Europe*, ch. 22; *History of All Nations*, XIX, ch. 4; Jamison and

62. Consolidation of the Italian Nation

OTHERS, *Italy Mediæval and Modern*, pp. 236–471; OGG, *Governments of Europe*, ch. 28; PHILLIPS, *Modern Europe, 1815-1899*, ch. 15; THAYER, *The Dawn of Italian Independence, 1814-1849*.

Source Readings:
McBAIN AND ROGERS, *The New Constitutions of Europe*, pp. 550–560; ROBINSON, *Readings in European History*, II, pp. 572–579; ROBINSON AND BEARD, *Readings in Modern European History*, II, pp. 115–131.

62. **Consolidation of the Italian Nation.**
   a. Completion of Italian Unification.
      i. The acquisition of Venetia, 1866.
      ii. The seizure of Rome, 1870.
      iii. Cavour's triumph: relations with France.
   b. The Rise of Domestic Problems.
      i. The "Prisoner of the Vatican."
         (a) Law of Papal Guarantees.
         (b) Relations between Papacy and Kingdom.
      ii. The suffrage problem: constitutional change.
         (a) Need of educational and social reform: illiteracy.
         (b) The trend toward democratic government.
   c. The Industrial Revolution in Italy.
      i. Lack of capital: German penetration.
      ii. Organization of labor: results.
      iii. Increase of sectional feeling.
         (a) Contrast between North and South.
         (b) Growing suspicion: effect on war patriotism.

Turner, *Europe Since 1789*, pp. 283-288.

Parallel References:
HAYES, *Political and Social History of Modern Europe*, II, pp. 174–175, 367–373
HAZEN, *Europe Since 1815*, pp. 369–378.
HAZEN, *Modern Europe*, pp. 508–511.
ROBINSON AND BEARD, *Development of Modern Europe*, II, pp. 99–102.
SCHAPIRO, *Modern and Contemporary European History*, pp. 218–219, 442–458.
SCHEVILL, *Political History of Modern Europe*, pp. 466–467, 502–504.

63. Recent National Issues in Italy

Supplementary References:
Cambridge Modern History, **XI**, ch. 19; **XII**, ch. 8; *History of All Nations*, XVII, ch. 2; HOLLAND, *Builders of United Italy*; JAMISON and OTHERS, *Italy, Mediæval and Modern*, pp. 472–500; MUNRO, *Governments of Europe*, ch. 34; OGG, *Economic Development of Modern Europe*, pp. 470–471, 562–564, 636–637; OGG, *Governments of Europe*, ch. 29; UNDERWOOD, *United Italy*, chs. 297–8; WALLACE, *Greater Italy*, chs. 2–7.

Source Readings:
MCBAIN AND ROGERS, *The New Constitutions of Europe*, pp. 561–564; ROBINSON, *Readings in European History*, II, pp. 579–580; ROBINSON AND BEARD, *Readings in Modern European History*, II, pp. 131–141.

63. Recent National Issues in Italy.

a. Trend of Foreign Policy.
  i. Italy and the Triple Alliance.
    (a) Colonial rivalry with France.
    (b) Diplomacy of Bismarck.
  ii. Progress of the Expansion Policy.
    (a) Colonial efforts: success: cost.
    (b) The shadow of *Italia Irredenta*.
  iii. The War with Turkey: results.
b. Italy in the World War.
  i. Motives for joining the *Entente*.
  ii. Narrow escape from disaster: Caporetto.
  iii. Acquisitions at the Peace Conference.
c. Post-War Issues.
  i. Problems of economic reconstruction.
  ii. The socialist movement: bolshevism.
  iii. Experiments with Fascism: Mussolini.

Turner, *Europe Since 1789*, pp. 288–289, 380–385, 493, 694–697, 722–724, *passim*.

Parallel References:
FUETER, *World History, 1815–1920*, pp. 431 *f.*, 464–468, 347–350.
HAYES, *Political and Social History of Modern Europe*, II, pp. 373–378.
HAZEN, *Europe Since 1815*, pp. 1021–1041.
HAZEN, *Modern Europe*, pp. 511–514.
HOLT AND CHILTON, *European History, 1862–1914*, pp. 255–260.

64. Prussian Assumption of German Leadership

ROBINSON AND BEARD, *Development of Modern Europe*, II, pp. 102–107.

SCHAPIRO, *Modern and Contemporary European History*, pp. 685–686, 730–731.

Supplementary References:
BOWMAN, *The New World*, ch. 5; GIBBONS, *The New Map of Europe*, ch. 7; *History of All Nations*, XX, chs. 2, 6; KING AND OAKLEY, *Italy Today*; Low, *Italy and the War*; MUNRO, *Governments of Europe*, ch. 35; OGG, *Governments of Europe*, ch. 30; POWERS, *Things Men Fight For*, ch. 15; UNDERWOOD, *United Italy*, chs. 3–6, 9–15; WALLACE, *Greater Italy*, chs. 8–12.

Source Readings:
New York *Times*, *Current History*, recent issues.

B. REALIGNMENT OF THE GERMAN STATES.

64. Prussian Assumption of German Leadership.
a. Growth of Prussian Prestige in Germany.
  i. Prussian fitness for leadership: government.
  ii. Formation of the *Zollverein*.
    (a) Advantages of the customs union.
    (b) Beginnings and growth of economic unity.
b. Internal Development of Prussia.
  i. Important military reforms.
  ii. Bismarck and the "Blood and Iron" policy.
c. The Austro-Prussian War.
  i. Causes of friction: Schleswig-Holstein.
  ii. The Seven Weeks' War: outcome.
  iii. Dissolution of the Germanic Confederation.
d. The North German Confederation.
  i. Character of the central government: constitution.
  ii. Effect on the Balance of Power.

Turner, *Europe Since 1789*, pp. 251–252, 259–266.

Parallel References:
FUETER, *World History, 1815–1920*, pp. 261–314.
HAYES, *Political and Social History of Modern Europe*, II, pp. 180–186.
HAZEN, *Europe Since 1815*, pp. 208–232.
HAZEN, *Modern Europe*, pp. 435–444.
HOLT AND CHILTON, *European History, 1862–1914*, pp. 60–116.

65. Establishment of the German Empire

Robinson and Beard, *Development of Modern Europe*, II, pp. 109–118.
Schapiro, *Modern and Contemporary European History*, pp. 115–130, 169–184.
Schevill, *Political History of Modern Europe*, pp. 468–474.

Supplementary References:
Cambridge Modern History, XI, ch. 15; Fyffe, *History of Modern Europe*, ch. 23; *History of All Nations*, XIX, chs. 1–2, 6–7; Henderson, *Short History of Germany*, II, ch. 9; Howard, *The German Empire*, ch. 1; Malleson, *The Refounding of the German Empire*; Marriott and Robertson, *The Evolution of Prussia*, chs. 9–11; Ogg, *Economic Development of Modern Europe*, pp. 218–231, ch. 4; Ogg, *Governments of Europe*, ch. 34; Phillips, *Modern Europe, 1815–1899*, ch. 16; Schevill, *The Making of Modern Germany*, chs. 1–4.

Source Readings:
Robinson, *Readings in European History*, II, pp. 580–588; Robinson and Beard, *Readings in Modern European History*, II, pp. 142–157.

65. Establishment of the German Empire.

a. Obstacles to German Unification.
  i. Attitude of other states: France.
  ii. Sectionalism and jealousy in Germany.
b. Rise of Franco-Prussian Difficulties.
  i. French demands for "compensation."
  ii. The diplomatic isolation of France.
  iii. Mutual preparations for war.
c. Trial by Combat.
  i. Jingoism in France: tne Ems Dispatch.
  ii. Alignment of German states: national spirit.
  iii. Course of the War: German successes: Sedan.
  iv. The siege of Paris: end of the War.
d. Formation of the Empire.
  i. Proclamation of the Empire at Versailles.
  ii. The Treaty of Frankfort: harsh terms.
  iii. Constitution of the Empire: Prussian dominance.
  iv. The operation of governmental machinery.

Turner, *Europe Since 1789*, pp. 266–267, 337–352.

Parallel References:
Hayes, *Political and Social History of Modern Europe*, II, pp. 186–206, 397–403.

66. Early Progress of the German State

Hazen, *Europe Since 1815*, pp. 243-256.
Hazen, *Modern Europe*, pp. 455-463.
Holt and Chilton, *European History, 1862-1914*, pp. 117-165.
Robinson and Beard, *Development of Modern Europe*, II, pp. 118-123, 130-136.
Schapiro, *Modern and Contemporary European History*, pp. 184-194.
Schevill, *Political History of Modern Europe*, pp. 474-479.

Supplementary References:
Cambridge Modern History, XI, chs. 16, 21; Fyffe, *History of Modern Europe*, ch. 24; Hazen, *Alsace-Lorraine under German Rule;* Henderson, *Short History of Germany*, ch. 10; *History of All Nations*, XIX, ch. 9; XX, ch. 5; Howard, *The German Empire*, chs. 1, 13; Marriott and Robertson, *The Evolution of Prussia*, ch. 12; Ogg, *Governments of Europe*, chs. 35-36; Phillips, *Modern Europe, 1815-1899*, chs. 17-18; Schevill, *The Making of Modern Germany*, ch. 5.

Source Readings:
Anderson, *Constitutions and Documents*, pp. 158-165, 176-177;
Robinson, *Readings in European History*, II, pp. 588-598;
Robinson and Beard, *Readings in Modern European History*, II, pp. 158-165, 176-177.

C. RECENT COURSE OF THE CENTRAL POWERS.

66. Early Progress of the German State.
a. Consolidation of the New Government.
   i. Establishment of Prussian authority: methods.
   ii. Representation in imperial government.
   iii. Increase in material prosperity: protective tariffs.
   iv. New and important legislation.
b. The Test of Imperial Authority.
   i. Religious troubles: the *Kulturkampf*.
      (a) Reasons for the conflict.
      (b) Bismarck's defeat: Catholic strength.
   ii. Rise of the Socialist Party.
      (a) Attempts to destroy the party.
      (b) The policy of "State Socialism."
c. Early Reign of Wilhelm II.
   i. His ambitions: retirement of Bismarck.
   ii. Increasing degree of personal government.
   iii. Reliance on military and naval policies.

Turner, *Europe Since 1789*, pp. 353-390.

67. The Course of Pan-Germanism

Parallel References:
FUETER, *World History, 1815–1920*, pp. 395–402.
HAYES, *Political and Social History of Modern Europe*, II, pp. 404–421.
HAZEN, *Europe Since 1815*, pp. 282–296.
HAZEN, *Modern Europe*, pp. 462–468.
HOLT AND CHILTON, *European History, 1862–1914*, pp. 166–184, 264–270.
ROBINSON AND BEARD, *Development of Modern Europe*, II, pp. 136–147.
SCHAPIRO, *Modern and Contemporary European History*, pp. 277–285, 288–310, 586–590.
SCHEVILL, *Political History of Modern Europe*, pp. 508–512.

Supplementary References:
BARKER, *The Foundations of Germany*, chs. 1–3; *Cambridge Modern History*, XII, ch. 6; DAWSON, *The Evolution of Modern Germany*, chs. 1–12, *passim; History of All Nations*, XIX, chs. 10–13; XX, ch. 6; HOWARD, *The German Empire*, chs. 2–9; MARRIOTT AND ROBERTSON, *The Evolution of Prussia*, ch. 13; OGG, *Economic Development of Modern Europe*, chs. 22, 24, pp. 450–456; OGG, *Governments of Europe*, ch. 36; ROSE, *The Development of the European Nations, 1870–1914*, pt. I, ch. 6; SCHEVILL, *The Making of Modern Germany*, pp. 159–177.

67. **The Course of Pan-Germanism.**
   a. The German Expansion Program.
      i. Relation of German industrialism and colonialism.
      ii. Methods of colonial acquisition.
      iii. Rise of an imperialistic attitude.
      iv. Character of colonial possessions.
         (a) The Chinese Expedition of 1897: Kiau Chau.
         (b) Occupation of island groups.
         (c) German spoils from the partition of Africa.
   b. The Inevitable Growth of Militarism.
      i. Prussian military tradition.
      ii. Beginnings of navalism: rivalry with Britain.
      iii. Foreign policy: "mailed fist" diplomacy.
      iv. Bearing on the World War.
   c. Results of German Defeat.
      i. Character of the German Republic: constitution.
      ii. Loss of territory: financial bankruptcy.
      iii. International aid in German rehabilitation.

Turner, *Europe Since 1789*, pp. 390-405, 523-525.

68. Nationalism in the Hapsburg Monarchy

Parallel References:
FUETER, *World History, 1815–1920*, pp. 325–327, 339–342, 395–402, *passim.*
HAYES, *Political and Social History of Modern Europe*, II, pp. 421–426, 507, 549, 621 *f.*, 633–636, 770–776, 855–860.
HAZEN, *Europe Since 1815*, pp. 297–330.
HAZEN, *Modern Europe*, pp. 468–481.
HOLT AND CHILTON, *European History, 1862–1914*, pp. 271–279, 524–538.
ROBINSON AND BEARD, *Development of Modern Europe*, II, pp. 147–150.
SCHAPIRO, *Modern and Contemporary European History*, pp. 285–287, 310–323.

Supplementary References:
BARKER, *The Foundations of Germany*, chs. 4–8; BOWMAN, *The New World*, ch. 10; BÜLOW, *Imperial Germany*; GIBBONS, *The New Map of Europe*, chs. 1–3; GOOCH, *History of Modern Europe, 1878–1919*, pp. 178–231; HOWARD, *The German Empire*, chs. 10–12; JASTROW, *The War and the Bagdad Railway*, pp. 82–121; MARRIOTT AND ROBERTSON, *The Evolution of Prussia*, ch. 14; MUNRO, *Governments of Europe*, chs. 32–33; OGG, *The Governments of Europe*, chs. 37–39; POWERS, *Things Men Fight For*, ch. 12; SCHEVILL, *The Making of Modern Germany*, pp. 177–206; YOUNG, *The New Germany*. See contemporary literature, such as New York *Times*, *Current History*, *Literary Digest*, etc.

Source Readings:
Documents in *International Conciliation*, and *League of Nations*; MCBAIN AND ROGERS, *The New Constitutions of Europe*, pp. 176–212; ROBINSON AND BEARD, *Readings in Modern European History*, II, pp. 193–207.

68. **Nationalism in the Hapsburg Monarchy.**
   a. Shrinking of the Hapsburg Domain.
      i. Austria's recovery from mid-century revolutions.
      ii. Loss of Italian territory in 1859.
      iii. Effects of the Austro-Prussian War.
   b. Establishment of the Dual Monarchy.
      i. Races and nationalities of the Austrian Empire.
      ii. The Compromise (*Ausgleich*) of 1867: reasons.
         (a) Political relation of the component states.
         (b) Character of central and local government.
      iii. The question of minor nationalities.

69. The Second Napoleonic Empire

c. Course of the Austrian Empire.
   i. Readjustment of internal machinery.
   ii. Liberal policy of Francis Joseph I.
   iii. Aggressive policy in the Balkans.
d. Austria in the Great War.
   i. The issues of 1914.
   ii. Disintegration of the Empire: new states.

Turner, *Europe Since 1789*, pp. 241-244, 268-269, 477-484, 724-726.

Parallel References:
FUETER, *World History, 1815–1920*, pp. 248–258, 403–471.
HAYES, *Political and Social History of Modern Europe*, II, pp. 426–435.
HAZEN, *Europe Since 1815*, pp. 379–393.
HAZEN, *Modern Europe*, pp. 515–526.
HOLT AND CHILTON, *European History, 1862–1914*, pp. 37–43, 261–264, 425–437.
ROBINSON AND BEARD, *Development of Modern Europe*, II, pp. 123–129.
SCHAPIRO, *Modern and Contemporary European History*, pp. 424–441.
SCHEVILL, *Political History of Modern Europe*, pp. 512–515.

Supplementary References:
BOWMAN, *The New World*, ch. 11; *Cambridge Modern History*, XII, ch. 7; DRAGE, *Austria-Hungary*, chs. 12–15; GIBBONS, *The New Map of Europe*, ch. 9; MUNRO, *Governments of Europe*, ch. 38, *passim;* POWERS, *Things Men Fight For*, ch. 10; STEED, *The Hapsburg Monarchy;* TOYNBEE, *Nationality and the War*, chs. 3–6; WHITMAN, *Austria*, chs. 22–24; WHITMAN, *The Realm of the Hapsburgs, passim.*

Source Readings:
MCBAIN AND ROGERS, *The New Constitutions of Europe*, pp. 241–306; ROBINSON AND BEARD, *Readings in Modern European History*, II, pp. 165–175.

X. WAVES OF LIBERALISM AND DEMOCRACY

A. THE RISE OF A DEMOCRATIC FRANCE.

69. The Second Napoleonic Empire.

a. Course of the Second French Republic.
   i. History of the provisional government.
   ii. The National Constituent Assembly: its work.

70. Early Vicissitudes of the Third Republic

  b. Rise of Louis Napoleon Bonaparte.
     i. Louis Napoleon as President.
     ii. The *coup d'état:* dawn of the Second Empire.
  c. Foreign Policy of the Emperor.
     i. The Crimean and Italian Wars: barren results.
     ii. Intervention in Mexico.
     iii. Alienation of support at home and abroad.
  d. The Decline of Napoleonic Prestige.
     i. The sham of liberal government.
     ii. Luxury of the royal court.
     iii. Plans for a popular military stroke.
     iv. French defeat, 1870: ruin of the Empire.

Turner, *Europe Since 1789,* pp. 225-233.

Parallel References:
Hayes, *Political and Social History of Modern Europe,* II, pp. 149–163, 175–180.
Hazen, *Europe Since 1815,* pp. 166–187, 233–242.
Hazen, *Modern Europe,* pp. 407–418, 445–457.
Holt and Chilton, *European History, 1862–1914,* pp. 53–59.
Robinson and Beard, *Development of Modern Europe,* II, pp. 63–71.
Schapiro, *Modern and Contemporary European History,* pp. 103–114, 145–168.
Schevill, *Political History of Modern Europe,* pp. 458–462.

Supplementary References:
Cambridge Modern History, XI, chs. 10, 17; Evans, *The Second French Empire;* Hassal, *France, Mediæval and Modern,* ch. 15; *History of All Nations,* XIX, chs. 2, 5, 8; Ogg, *Governments of Europe,* ch. 20; Phillips, *Modern Europe, 1815–1899,* ch. 14; Rose, *The Development of the European Nations, 1871–1914,* pt. I, ch. 1; Wright, *History of the Third French Republic,* ch. 1.

Source Readings:
Anderson, *Constitutions and Documents,* pp. 538–592; Robinson and Beard, *Readings in Modern European History,* II, pp. 155–163.

70. Early Vicissitudes of the Third Republic.

  a. Origin: The Franco-German War.
     i. Diplomacy of the War.
     ii. Downfall of the monarchy.

70. Early Vicissitudes of the Third Republic

    iii. Provisional basis of the new order.
    iv. Peace with the Germans: Frankfort.
    v. The "Commune" episode in Paris.

b. French Recovery and Consolidation.
    i. The National Assembly: party groups.
    ii. The Chambord incident.
    iii. The Organic Laws.
        (a) Basis of permanent order.
        (b) Nature of the new parliamentary government.
    iv. Payment of the German indemnity.

c. Tests of the New Government.
    i. Growth of material prosperity.
    ii. Social legislation: education.
    iii. The Boulanger episode.
    iv. Importance of the Dreyfus case.

Turner, *Europe Since 1789*, pp. 406–417.

Parallel References:
Fueter, *World History, 1815–1920*, II, pp. 382–391.
Hayes, *Political and Social History of Modern Europe*, II, pp. 199–206, 352–358.
Hazen, *Europe Since 1815*, pp. 331–359.
Hazen, *Modern Europe*, pp. 483–499.
Holt and Chilton, *European History, 1862–1914*, pp. 237–241, 290–292.
Robinson and Beard, *Development of Modern Europe*, II, pp. 151–166.
Schapiro, *Modern and Contemporary European History*, pp. 197–204.
Schevill, *Political and Social History of Modern Europe*, pp. 504–508.

Supplementary References:
Bracq, *France under the Third Republic; Cambridge Modern History*, XII, ch. 5; Hassal, *France, Mediæval and Modern*, pp. 270–277; *History of All Nations*, XX, chs. 1, 7; Ogg, *Governments of Europe*, ch. 21; Rose, *The Development of the European Nations, 1871–1914*, pt. I, chs. 4–5; Vizetelly, *Republican France, 1870–1912*; Wright, *History of the Third French Republic*, chs. 2–7.

Source Readings:
Anderson, *Constitutions and Documents*, pp. 592–650; McBain and Rogers, *The New Constitutions of Europe*, pp. 521–549;

71. **French Problems in Democratic Government**

ROBINSON AND BEARD, *Readings in Modern European History*, II, pp. 521–549.

71. **French Problems in Democratic Government.**
   a. The Separation of Church and State.
      i. Growth of religious orders: clerical power.
      ii. Repeal of the Concordat: separation legislation.
   b. Origin and Alignment of Political Parties.
      i. The group system of party action.
      ii. Political issues and "blocs."
         (a) Rapid growth of socialism.
         (b) Clashes over reform legislation.
      iii. Comparison of French and English democracies.
   c. The Expansion of France.
      i. Motives for colonialism and imperialism.
      ii. Fields of French colonizing activities.
      iii. International aspects: formation of the Entente.
   d. Recent Foreign and Domestic Issues.
      i. The Peace: French occupation of the Ruhr.
      ii. Policies of internal reconstruction: finances.

Turner, *Europe Since 1789*, pp. 417-429, 673-674, 677-685, 731.

Parallel References:
FUETER, *World History, 1815–1920*, pp. 112–128, 381–382.
HAYES, *Political and Social History of Modern Europe*, II, pp. 331–352, 358–367, ch. 21.
HAZEN, *Europe Since 1815*, pp. 359–368, 946–961.
HAZEN, *Modern Europe*, pp. 499–507.
HOLT AND CHILTON, *European History, 1862–1914*, pp. 292–293, 411–420, 518–524.
ROBINSON AND BEARD, *Development of Modern Europe*, II, pp. 166–179.
SCHAPIRO, *Modern and Contemporary European History*, pp. 235–248, 257–276.
SCHEVILL, *Political History of Modern Europe*, pp. 507–508, *passim*.

Supplementary References:
BOWMAN, *The New World*, ch. 3; BUELL, *Contemporary French Politics*; HASSAL, *France, Mediæval and Modern*, pp. 277-293; GOOCH, *History of Modern Europe, 1878–1919*, pp. 264–297; MUNRO, *Governments of Europe*, chs. 21–28; OGG, *Economic Development of Modern Europe*, pp. 458–469; OGG, *Governments of Europe*, chs. 22–27; POINCARÉ, *How France Is Governed;*

72. Abolition of the Old Régime

POWERS, *Things Men Fight For*, ch. 14; WRIGHT, *History of the Third French Republic*, chs. 8–10.

Source Readings:
ANDERSON, *Constitutions and Documents*, pp. 650–681; ROBINSON AND BEARD, *Readings in Modern European History*, II, pp. 224–238.

B. A CENTURY OF REFORM IN ENGLAND.

72. **Abolition of the Old Régime.**
   a. The Problem of 1830.
      i. The old system of representation.
         (a) Parliamentary elections: "rotten" and "pocket" boroughs.
         (b) Privilege and monopoly in local government.
         (c) Diversity of conditions: lack of real representation.
      ii. Social and economic discontent.
         (a) Religious abuses: disabilities of non-conformists.
         (b) Industrial factors: ignorance and poverty.
      iii. Rise of reform sentiment.
      iv. Reaction from the French Revolution.
   b. First Steps toward Popular Government.
      i. The Reform Bills of 1831: failure.
      ii. Passage of the Bill of 1832: the "safety valve."
         (a) Effect of popular agitation.
         (b) Readjustments involved in the measure.
      iii. Contemporary social reforms: slavery.
      iv. Changes in local government: Act of 1835.

Turner, *Europe Since 1789*, pp. 148–186.

Parallel References:
FUETER, *World History, 1815–1920*, p. 82, *passim*.
HAYES, *Political and Social History of Modern Europe*, II, pp. 100–110.
HAZEN, *Europe Since 1815*, pp. 394–423.
HAZEN, *Modern Europe*, pp. 339–355.
ROBINSON AND BEARD, *Development of Modern Europe*, II, 181–187, 198–199, 201–206.
SCHAPIRO, *Modern and Contemporary European History*, pp. 45–66.
SCHEVILL, *Political History of Modern Europe*, pp. 480–484.

73. Extension of the Reform Movement

Supplementary References:
Cambridge Modern History, X, chs. 18–19; CHEYNEY, *Short History of England*, pp. 617–632; CROSS, *History of England and Greater Britain*, chs. 49–50; HULME, *History of the British People*, ch. 24; LARSON, *History of England and the British Commonwealth*, ch. 22; SLATER, *The Making of Modern England*, chs. 1–9; TREVELYAN, *British History in the Nineteenth Century*, chs. 1–2, 4, 12–15.

Source Readings:
CHEYNEY, *Readings in English History*, pp. 663–702; ROBINSON AND BEARD, *Readings in Modern European History*, II, pp. 239–249, 267–286.

73. Extension of the Reform Movement.
a. The Chartist Agitation.
  i. Relation to contemporary political movements.
  ii. Program and methods of the Chartists: significance.
b. Changes in English Economic Policy.
  i. Origin and nature of the corn laws.
  ii. Organized opposition: the Anti-Corn Law League.
  iii. Irish famine: belated adoption of free trade.
c. Further Political Reform.
  i. Suffrage demands: the Bill of 1866.
  ii. The Reform Bill of 1867: provisions.
d. Rise of the Irish Question.
e. Miscellaneous Reform Legislation.
f. Imperialism in Foreign Policy.
  i. Intervention in Egypt: financial control.
  ii. Purchase of the Suez Canal shares.
  iii. Disraeli and the Berlin Congress (1878): Cyprus.

Turner, *Europe Since 1789*, pp. 186–207.

Parallel References:
FUETER, *World History, 1815–1920*, pp. 95 f., 171, *passim*.
HAYES, *Political and Social History of Modern Europe*, II, pp. 110–116, 307–309, 319–321.
HAZEN, *Europe Since 1815*, pp. 423–438.
HAZEN, *Modern Europe*, pp. 355–364.
HOLT AND CHILTON, *European History, 1862–1914*, pp. 226–228.
ROBINSON AND BEARD, *Development of Modern Europe*, II, 187–193, 206–218.

74. The Close of the Victorian Era

Schapiro, *Modern and Contemporary European History,* pp. 66–88.
Schevill, *Political History of Modern Europe,* pp. 485–486 (inadequate).

Supplementary References:
Cambridge Modern History, X, chs. 23–24; XI, ch. 1; Cheyney, *Short History of England,* pp. 632–662; Cross, *History of England and Greater Britain,* chs. 51–54; Hulme, *History of the British People,* ch. 25; *History of All Nations,* XVIII, ch. 11; XIX, ch. 3; Larson, *History of England and the British Commonwealth,* ch. 23; Ogg, *Governments of Europe,* pp. 242–250; Slater, *The Making of Modern England,* chs. 11–16; Trevelyan, *British History in the Nineteenth Century,* chs. 17–23; Webster, *General History of Commerce,* ch. 23.

Source Readings:
Cheyney, *Readings in English History,* pp. 702–752; Robinson and Beard, *Readings in Modern European History,* II, pp. 249–254, 287–297.

74. The Close of the Victorian Era.
a. Further Constitutional Changes.
   i. The Reform Bills of 1884 and 1885.
   ii. Extent and equalization of the franchise.
b. New and Far-Reaching Reform Legislation.
   i. The passage of Factory and Mines Acts.
   ii. Improvements in education.
   iii. Labor reforms: workingmen's compensation.
   iv. The land problem and the income tax.
c. Party Issues and Party Changes.
   i. The Irish Home Rule problem.
      (a) The Irish land question: origin.
      (b) Gladstone's championship of the Irish cause.
      (c) The religious situation: Church disestablishment.
   ii. Party alignment on critical issues.
      (a) The failure of Irish Home Rule measures.
      (b) Party differences on foreign policy: South Africa.
      (c) Split of the liberal party: Liberal Unionists.

Turner, *Europe Since 1789,* pp. 430–442.

Parallel References:
Fueter, *World History, 1815–1920,* pp. 165–186, *passim.*
Hayes, *Political and Social History of Modern Europe,* II, pp. 277–288, 307–313, 321–326.

75. Perfecting of Cabinet Government

HAZEN, *Europe Since 1815*, pp. 439-463.
HAZEN, *Modern Europe*, pp. 527-552.
HOLT AND CHILTON, *European History, 1862-1914*, pp. 228-237.
ROBINSON AND BEARD, *Development of Modern Europe*, II, pp. 192-193, 199-200, 218-232.
SCHAPIRO, *Modern and Contemporary European History*, pp. 328-362.
SCHEVILL, *Political History of Modern Europe*, pp. 486-490.

Supplementary References:
Cambridge Modern History, XI, chs. 3, 11-12; CHEYNEY, *Short History of England*, pp. 662-679; CROSS, *History of England and Greater Britain*, chs. 55-56; *History of All Nations*, XX, ch. 3; HULME, *History of the British People*, ch. 26; LARSON, *History of England and the British Commonwealth*, chs. 24-26; OGG, *Economic Development of Modern Europe*, ch. 17; SLATER, *The Making of Modern England*, chs. 16-19; TREVELYAN, *British History in the Nineteenth Century*, chs. 24-25.

Source Readings:
CHEYNEY, *Readings in English History*, pp. 768-778; HAYES, *British Social Politics*, chs. 1-4; ROBINSON AND BEARD, *Readings in Modern European History*, II, pp. 255-258, 297-305.

75. **Perfecting of Cabinet Government.**
 a. Curbing of the House of Lords.
    i. Obstruction of the Budget of 1909.
    ii. The Parliament Act of 1911: importance.
 b. Attainment of Political Democracy.
    i. Recent progress in popular education.
    ii. The suffrage measures of 1918.
        (a) Culmination of the Woman Suffrage movement.
        (b) Broad scope of this Act.
 c. Rise of the Labor Party.
    i. Its origin and growth: Sidney and Beatrice Webb.
    ii. Accession to power: character of program.
    iii. Return to Conservative government.
 d. The Composition and Functioning of Parliament.
    i. Flexible nature of the British Constitution.
    ii. Working of the representative system.
    iii. The Cabinet System: position of the Sovereign.
        (a) Joint responsibility: departments.
        (b) Emergency organization: the War Cabinet.

76. Autocratic Policies: Reform and Reaction

e. Fundamentals of Foreign Policy.

Turner, *Europe Since 1789*, pp. 442-454.

Parallel References:
FUETER, *World History, 1815-1920*, pp. 393-395.
HAYES, *Political and Social History of Modern Europe*, II, pp. 288-307, 313-319.
HAZEN, *Europe Since 1815*, pp. 464-485, 962-994.
HAZEN, *Modern Europe*, pp. 552-561.
HOLT AND CHILTON, *European History, 1862-1914*, pp. 388-410, 511-518.
ROBINSON AND BEARD, *Development of Modern Europe*, II, pp. 193-198.
SCHAPIRO, *Modern and Contemporary European History*, pp. 324-328, 362-381.

Supplementary References:
ALDEN, *Democratic England; Cambridge Modern History*, XII, ch. 3; CHEYNEY, *Short History of England*, ch. 21; CROSS, *History of England and Greater Britain*, ch. 57; *History of All Nations*, XX, ch. 8; HULME, *History of the British People*, ch. 27; LARSON, *History of England and the British Commonwealth*, chs. 27-28; LOW, *The Governance of England*; MUNRO, *Governments of Europe*, chs. 3-9; OGG, *Economic Development of Modern Europe*, ch. 19; OGG, *Governments of Europe*, chs. 4-18; POWERS, *Things Men Fight For*, ch. 13; SLATER, *The Making of Modern England*, chs. 20-23.

Source Readings:
CHEYNEY, *Readings in English History*, pp. 799-834; HAYES, *British Social Politics*, chs. 5-10; MCBAIN AND ROGERS, *The New Constitutions of Europe*, pp. 573-601; ROBINSON AND BEARD, *Readings in Modern European History*, II, pp. 258-266.

C. DECLINE OF MEDIEVALISM IN RUSSIA.

76. Autocratic Policies: Reform and Reaction.
a. Changing Policies of Russian Autocrats.
   i. Alexander I: from liberalism to reaction.
   ii. The despotism of Nicholas I.
   iii. The emancipation of the serfs: illusions.
      (a) Alexander II and the Emancipation Edict: 1861.
      (b) The subsequent land problem: the *mir*.
      (c) Continuation of economic slavery.

77. Growth of Social and Political Unrest
  b. The Return to Repression.
    i. Reactionary measures of Alexander II.
    ii. Rise of Nihilism: the "Third Section."
    iii. Autocracy of Alexander III.
      (a) Repressive measures: success.
      (b) "Russification" of non-Russian minorities.
  c. Character of Russian Foreign Policy.
    i. Relation to the need of open ports.
    ii. Stakes of the Crimean War.
    iii. Subsequent troubles with Turkey.

Turner, *Europe Since 1789*, pp. 291-316.

Parallel References:
  FUETER, *World History, 1815-1920*, pp. 219 ff., 417, passim.
  HAYES, *Political and Social History of Modern Europe*, II, pp. 452-473.
  HAZEN, *Europe Since 1815*, pp. 581-608.
  HAZEN, *Modern Europe*, pp. 628-639.
  HOLT AND CHILTON, *European History, 1862-1914*, pp. 49-52, 241-246, 293-294.
  ROBINSON AND BEARD, *Development of Modern Europe*, II, pp. 261-280.
  SCHAPIRO, *Modern and Contemporary European History*, pp. 499-542.
  SCHEVILL, *Political and Social History of Modern Europe*, pp. 491-493.

Supplementary References:
  BEAZLEY, FORBES, BIRKETT, *Russia from the Varangians to the Bolsheviks*, pp. 356-470; *Cambridge Modern History*, XII, ch. 12; MORFILL, *A History of Russia*, chs. 11-14; *History of All Nations*, XIX, ch. 3; XX, ch. 2; ROSE, *The Development of the European Nations, 1871-1914*, pt. I, ch. 11; SKRINE, *Expansion of Russia*, chs. 1-4; WALLACE, *Russia*, chs. 28-32.

Source Readings:
  ROBINSON AND BEARD, *Readings in Modern European History*, II, pp. 338-367.

77. Growth of Social and Political Unrest.
  a. Effects of the Russian Industrial Revolution.
    i. The growth of industry: new social problems.
    ii. Plans for economic emancipation: De Witte.
    iii. Commercial and colonial expansion: Siberia.

77. Growth of Social and Political Unrest

b. The Climax of Russian Autocracy.
   i. Causes of the Russo-Japanese War.
      (a) Rival interests in the Far East.
      (b) Comparative strength and preparedness.
   ii. Russian defeat: official scandals and their effects.
   iii. Spread of socialistic ideas.
c. Foreshadowing of the Revolutionary Upheaval.
   i. Political concessions of Nicholas II: the Duma.
   ii. The mirage of political reform: stultification.
   iii. The use of Terror as a reactionary measure.
   iv. Compromise between autocracy and popular government.
   v. Effects of the Great War.

Turner, *Europe Since 1789*, pp. 455-475.
Parallel References:
FUETER, *World History, 1815-1920*, pp. 129-139, 213-221, 356-358.
HAYES, *Political and Social History of Modern Europe*, II, pp. 473-487.
HAZEN, *Europe Since 1815*, pp. 609-636.
HAZEN, *Modern Europe*, pp. 639-641, 650-659.
HOLT AND CHILTON, *European History, 1862-1914*, pp. 420-425.
ROBINSON AND BEARD, *Development of Modern Europe*, II, pp. 280-302, 346-353.
SCHAPIRO, *Modern and Contemporary European History*, pp. 542-569.
SCHEVILL, *Political History of Modern Europe*, pp. 499-569.

Supplementary References:
ALEXINSKY, *Modern Russia, passim;* BEAZLEY, FORBES, BIRKETT, *Russia from the Varangians to the Bolsheviks*, pp. 470-557; BOWMAN, *The New World*, ch. 23; *Cambridge Modern History*, XII, chs. 13-14; GOOCH, *History of Modern Europe, 1878-1919*, pp. 23-32; HINDUS, *The Russian Peasant and the Revolution*, chs. 1-8; *History of All Nations*, XX, chs. 7, 11; MUNRO, *Governments of Europe*, ch. 37; OGG, *Economic Development of Modern Europe*, ch. 15; POWERS, *Things Men Fight For*, ch. 11; ROSE, *The Development of The European Nations, 1871-1914*, pt. II, ch. 9; SKRINE, *Expansion of Russia*, chs. 5-8; ULAR, *Russia from Within*.

Source Readings:
ROBINSON AND BEARD, *Readings in Modern European History*, II, pp. 368-381, 444-448.

78. Interests of the Powers in Balkan Liberation

XI. WORLD PROBLEMS AND ATTEMPTED SOLUTIONS

A. RECENT HISTORY OF THE NEAR EAST.

78. Interests of the Powers in Balkan Liberation.
   a. Evolution of the Serbian Principality.
      i. Early struggles of the Serbians.
      ii. Formation of a principality in 1830.
   b. The Greek War of Independence.
      i. Plight of the Greeks under Turkish rule.
      ii. Foreign intervention: creation of a kingdom.
   c. The Crimean War.
      i. Causes of the struggle: motives of the Great Powers.
      ii. Importance of the Treaty of Paris, 1856.
   d. Reopening of the Eastern Question.
      i. The Balkan War of 1876-1878: San Stefano.
      ii. Work of the Berlin Congress: revision.
   e. Development of Bulgaria and Rumania.
      i. Agitation in Bulgaria: Russian intervention.
      ii. Rise of the Rumanian Kingdom.
      iii. Alignment of the Great Powers.

Turner, *Europe Since 1789*, pp. 482-510.

Parallel References:
   FUETER, *World History, 1815-1920*, pp. 36-43, 212-222, 403-422.
   HAYES, *Political and Social History of Modern Europe*, II, pp. 162-163, 490-523.
   HAZEN, *Europe Since 1815*, pp. 552-580.
   HAZEN, *Modern Europe*, pp. 610-620.
   HOLT AND CHILTON, *European History, 1862-1914*, pp. 187-219, 246-254.
   ROBINSON AND BEARD, *Development of Modern Europe*, II, pp. 303-317.
   SCHAPIRO, *Modern and Contemporary European History*, pp. 621-640.
   SCHEVILL, *Political History of Modern Europe*, pp. 493-499.

Supplementary References:
   BOWMAN, *The New World*, chs. 14-17; *Cambridge Modern History*, XI, chs. 2, 9, 22; XII, ch. 14; DAVIS, *A Short History of*

79. The Turkish Revolution and the Balkan Wars

the Near East, chs. 26–30; GIBBONS, *The New Map of Europe*, ch. 10; GOOCH, *History of Modern Europe, 1878–1919*, pp. 1–23; *History of All Nations*, XX, ch. 9; MARRIOTT, *The Eastern Question*, chs. 10–13; MILLER, *The Ottoman Empire and Its Successors, 1801–1922*, chs. 3–16; POWERS, *Things Men Fight For*, ch. 9; ROSE, *The Development of the European Nations, 1871–1914*, pt. I, chs. 7–8.

Source Readings:
HOLLAND, *The European Concert in the Eastern Question*, pp. 335–350, 356–358; ROBINSON AND BEARD, *Readings in Modern European History*, II, pp. 382–400.

79. The Turkish Revolution and the Balkan Wars.

a. Internal Disruption of the Turkish Empire.
   i. The Young Turk movement.
   ii. The military revolt of 1908: Balkan participation.
b. Course of the New Turkish Régime: Complications.
   i. Austrian annexation of "occupied" provinces.
   ii. Renewed struggles of Balkan Christians.
   iii. Disagreements among the Great Powers.
   iv. The Turkish counter revolution: outcome.
c. The Turco-Italian War, 1911–1912.
   i. Dismemberment of the Turkish Empire: Libya.
   ii. Bearing on Balkan troubles and the Great War.
d. Series of Balkan Wars.
   i. The Balkan Alliance (1912) against Turkey.
   ii. The Partition of European Turkey.
      (a) Success of the Allies: Treaty of London.
      (b) Disagreement over the spoils.
   iii. War among the Allies (1913).
      (a) Factors in the Second Balkan War.
      (b) Unsatisfactory Treaty of Bucharest.

Turner, *Europe Since 1789*, pp. 487, 493-498, 538, 547-549.

Parallel References:
FUETER, *World History, 1815–1920*, pp. 412–420, *passim*.
HAYES, *Political and Social History of Modern Europe*, II, pp. 523–539.
HAZEN, *Europe Since 1815*, pp. 637–652.
HAZEN, *Modern Europe*, pp. 620–627, 660–677.
HOLT AND CHILTON, *European History, 1862–1914*, pp. 438–455, 477–511.

80. The Scope of the British Empire

ROBINSON AND BEARD, *Development of Modern Europe*, II, pp. 516–518, 532.
SCHAPIRO, *Modern and Contemporary European History*, pp. 640–649.
SCHEVILL, *Political History of Modern Europe*, pp. 556–562.

Supplementary References:
BOWMAN, *The New World*, chs. 18, 24, 26–28; DAVIS, *A Short History of the Near East*, chs. 31–35; EVERSLEY AND CHIROL, *The Turkish Empire from 1288–1922*, chs. 21–22; FORBES AND OTHERS, *The Balkans*, passim; GIBBONS, *The New Map of Europe*, chs. 11–17; GOOCH, *History of Modern Europe, 1878–1919*, chs. 4, 12, 15; *History of All Nations*, XX, chs. 4, 9; MARRIOTT, *The Eastern Question*, chs. 15–17; MILLER, *The Ottoman Empire and Its Successors, 1801–1922*, chs. 17–20; MOWRER, *Balkanized Europe*; POWERS, *Things Men Fight For*, chs. 5, 8; ROSE, *The Development of The European Nations, 1871–1914*, pt. I, chs. 9–10; SCHURMAN, *The Balkan Wars*.

Source Readings:
ROBINSON AND BEARD, *Readings in Modern European History*, II, pp. 400–405.

B. IMPERIALISM AND INTERNATIONAL DIPLOMACY.

80. The Scope of the British Empire.
a. The British Empire as a Trading Concern.
  i. The relation of expansion to commercialism.
  ii. Dominant motives and policies in British expansion.
b. Origin and Growth of the Dominions.
  i. The rise of British nations in Australasia, Africa, America.
    (a) Prevalence of British population.
    (b) Stages of political evolution common to all.
  ii. Recent imperial status of the Irish states.
  iii. Expansion of English language, culture, and wealth.
c. Character of Dependencies and Minor Colonies.
  i. Evolution of the Empire of India: key position.
  ii. The galaxy of lesser possessions.
  iii. British protectorates and spheres of influence.
d. The Empire in World Affairs.
  i. Its relation to international diplomacy.

81. Recent Phases of European Expansion
  ii. Projects for imperial federation.
  iii. The Empire as an agency for peace.

Turner, *Europe Since 1789,* pp. 513-521.

Parallel References:
  Fueter, *World History, 1815-1920,* pp. 103-111, 129-139, 154-186.
  Hayes, *Political and Social History of Modern Europe,* II, pp. 545-560, 640-675.
  Hazen, *Europe Since 1815,* pp. 486-508.
  Hazen, *Modern Europe,* pp. 563-582.
  Holt and Chilton, *European History, 1862-1914,* pp. 294-299.
  Robinson and Beard, *Development of Modern Europe,* II, pp. 233-260.
  Schapiro, *Modern and Contemporary European History,* pp. 399-423.
  Schevill, *Political History of Modern Europe,* pp. 487-490.

Supplementary References:
  Bowman, *The New World,* chs. 2, 25, 29, 32; *Cambridge Modern History,* X, ch. 20; XII, ch. 4; Cheyney, *Short History of England,* pp. 666-678, *passim;* Cross, *A History of England and Greater Britain,* pp. 1002-1008, 1028-1036, 1064 *ff.*; Gibbons, *The New Map of Africa,* chs. 1, 5, 10-11, 14, 21-23; Gooch, *History of Modern Europe, 1878-1919,* ch. 9; *History of All Nations,* XX, ch. 10; XXI, chs. 1-2; Larson, *History of England and the British Commonwealth,* chs. 25, 31; Muir, *The Expansion of Europe,* chs. 6-8; Munro, *Governments of Europe,* chs. 18-19; Ogg, *Governments of Europe,* ch. 19; Powers, *Things Men Fight For,* ch. 13; Slater, *The Making of Modern England,* ch. 22.

Source Readings:
  Cheyney, *Readings in English History,* pp. 752-767; Robinson and Beard, *Readings in Modern European History,* II, pp. 306-337; Scott, *Autonomy and Federation within Empire.*

81. Recent Phases of European Expansion.
  a. Forces and Factors in Nineteenth Century Expansion.
    i. Effects of the Industrial Revolution.
      (a) Improvement in means of communication.
      (b) Economic impulses in the expansion movement.

81. Recent Phases of European Expansion

      ii. Racial and environmental influences.
     iii. Relative fitness for expansion of European peoples.
  b. The Partition of Africa and of Asia.
      i. Methods and motives in African exploitation.
     ii. Rival possessions: extent and value.
    iii. European holdings in Asia: spheres of influence.
  c. The Europeanizing of the Modern World.
      i. Extent of European colonial interests.
     ii. Expansion of European cultures.
    iii. Europeanizing of the non-European world.
    iv. Resultant problems: political, social, economic.

Turner, *Europe Since 1789*, pp. 511-513, 528-531.

Parallel References:
Fueter, *World History, 1815–1920*, pp. 325–351.
Hayes, *Political and Social History of Modern Europe*, II, pp. 560–637.
Hazen, *Europe Since 1815*, pp. 509–519.
Hazen, *Modern Europe*, pp. 581–591, 642–650.
Holt and Chilton, *European History, 1862–1914*, pp. 317–364.
Robinson and Beard, *Development of Modern Europe*, II, pp. 318–361.
Schapiro, *Modern and Contemporary European History*, pp. 650–683.
Schevill, *Political History of Modern Europe*, pp. 542–547.

Supplementary References:
Beer, *African Questions at the Paris Peace Conference*, pts. 1–5; Bowman, *The New World*, chs. 3, 7, 23; *Cambridge Modern History*, XI, ch. 28; XII, ch. 17; Gibbons, *The New Map of Africa*, chs. 6–9, 12–13, 16–17; Gibbons, *The New Map of Europe*, ch. 5; Gooch, *History of Modern Europe, 1878–1919*, chs. 3, 13; *History of All Nations*, XXI, chs. 3–10; XII; XXIII; Johnston, *History of the Colonization of Africa by Alien Races*; Keltie, *The Partition of Africa*; Muir, *The Expansion of Europe*, chs. 1, 5, 9–10; Ogg, *Economic Development of Modern Europe*, ch. 16; Powers, *Things Men Fight For*, ch. 7; Webster, *General History of Commerce*, chs. 28–34.

Source Readings:
Beer, *African Questions at the Paris Peace Conference*, pp. 5–15*ff*.; Robinson, *Readings in European History*, II, pp. 620–621; Robinson and Beard, *Readings in Modern European History*, II, pp. 237–238, 406–444, 448–458.

82. The Balance of Power and the Alliances

82. **The Balance of Power and the Alliances.**
   a. The Congress of Berlin (1878).
      i. The Balkan situation: revision of the San Stefano treaty.
      ii. Blunders of the Congress: failure.
   b. Formation of New International Alliances.
      i. The alignment of Powers after 1870.
      ii. The Austro-Prussian Alliance: attachment of Italy.
      iii. The Franco-Russian Dual Alliance: basis.
      iv. Late evolution of the Triple Entente.
      v. Possibilities of a general European war.
         (a) Foci of trouble: Balkans, Africa, Asia.
         (b) Development of an armed neutrality.
   c. The Hague Peace Conferences.
      i. Sources of Peace Proposals.
      ii. The first Conference (1899): results.
      iii. Response to the second Conference (1907).
      iv. Limited accomplishments of peace attempts: reasons.

Turner, *Europe Since 1789*, pp. 532-537, 551-565, 795-796.

Parallel References:
Hayes, *Political and Social History of Modern Europe*, II, pp. 679-691.
Hazen, *Europe Since 1815*, pp. 295-296, 374-378, 637-640, 661-662, *passim*.
Hazen, *Modern Europe*, pp. 470-471, 495, 506-507, 685-687.
Holt and Chilton, *European History, 1862-1914*, pp. 207-225, 283-290.
Robinson and Beard, *Development of Modern Europe*, II, pp. 129, 311-312, 367-372.
Schapiro, *Modern and Contemporary European History*, pp. 684-699.
Schevill, *Political History of Modern Europe*, pp. 548-556.

Supplementary References:
Brandes, *The World at War*, pp. 1-31; Chitwood, *Furdamental Causes of the War;* Choate, *The Two Hague Conferences;* Coolidge, *The Origins of The Triple Alliance;* Davis, *The Roots of the War;* Gibbons, *The New Map of Africa*, ch. 6; Gooch,

83. The Prelude to War: Diplomatic Clashes

History of Modern Europe, 1878–1919, chs. 2, 5, 14; Powers, *Things Men Fight For*, chs. 1–2; Rose, *The Development of the European Nations, 1871–1914*, pt. II, chs. 1–2, 10; Tardieu, *France and the Alliances*.

Source Readings:
Cheyney, *Readings in English History*, pp. 804–806; McKinley, *Collected Materials for the Study of the War*, pts. 2–3; Robinson and Beard, *Readings in Modern European History*, II, pp. 396–399, 458–466.

83. The Prelude to War: Diplomatic Clashes.
a. The Basis of International Differences.
  i. The demands of German industry.
    (a) Late arrival in the colonial field.
    (b) Demands for "a place in the sun."
  ii. Frequent inadequacy of arbitration.
b. Critical Diplomatic Crises.
  i. Early difficulties in Morocco: Tangier and Casablanca.
  ii. The problem of Bosnia and Herzegovina.
  iii. Reopening of the Moroccan question: Agadir.
  iv. Effects of the Turco-Italian and Balkan wars.
  v. The ashes of bitterness: mutual grievances.
c. Militarism and War Preparations.
  i. Results of imperialism: the objects of war.
  ii. International competition in armaments.
  iii. Relative strength: Europe as an armed camp.

Turner, *Europe Since 1789*, pp. 537-550.

Parallel References:
Hayes, *Political and Social History of Modern Europe*, II, pp. 691–711.
Hazen, *Europe Since 1815*, pp. 366–368, 393, 571, 643, *passim*.
Hazen, *Modern Europe*, pp. 505–507, 526, 666, 670, 680, *passim*.
Holt and Chilton, *European History, 1862–1914*, pp. 299–316, 365–387, 456–474.
Robinson and Beard, *Development of Modern Europe*, II, pp. 361–363.
Schapiro, *Modern and Contemporary European History*, pp. 700–708.
Schevill, *Political History of Modern Europe*, pp. 500 *f.*